Expressive Techniques for Orchestra

by

Kathleen DeBerry
Brungard

Michael
Alexander

Sandra
Dackow

Gerald E.
Anderson

In Memory of Gerald E. Anderson

Our colleague and friend, Gerald Anderson, was a dedicated music educator, author and composer. His contributions to our field of string and orchestral music education will long be remembered and appreciated. His publications have guided and will continue to touch the lives of young musicians everywhere. This publication is dedicated to and published in his memory.

© Copyright 2011 by Tempo Press LLC, Madison Heights, MI.
International Copyright Secured. All Rights Reserved Including Public Performance for Profit.
Any copying arranging or adapting of this work without the owner's consent is an infringement of the copyright.

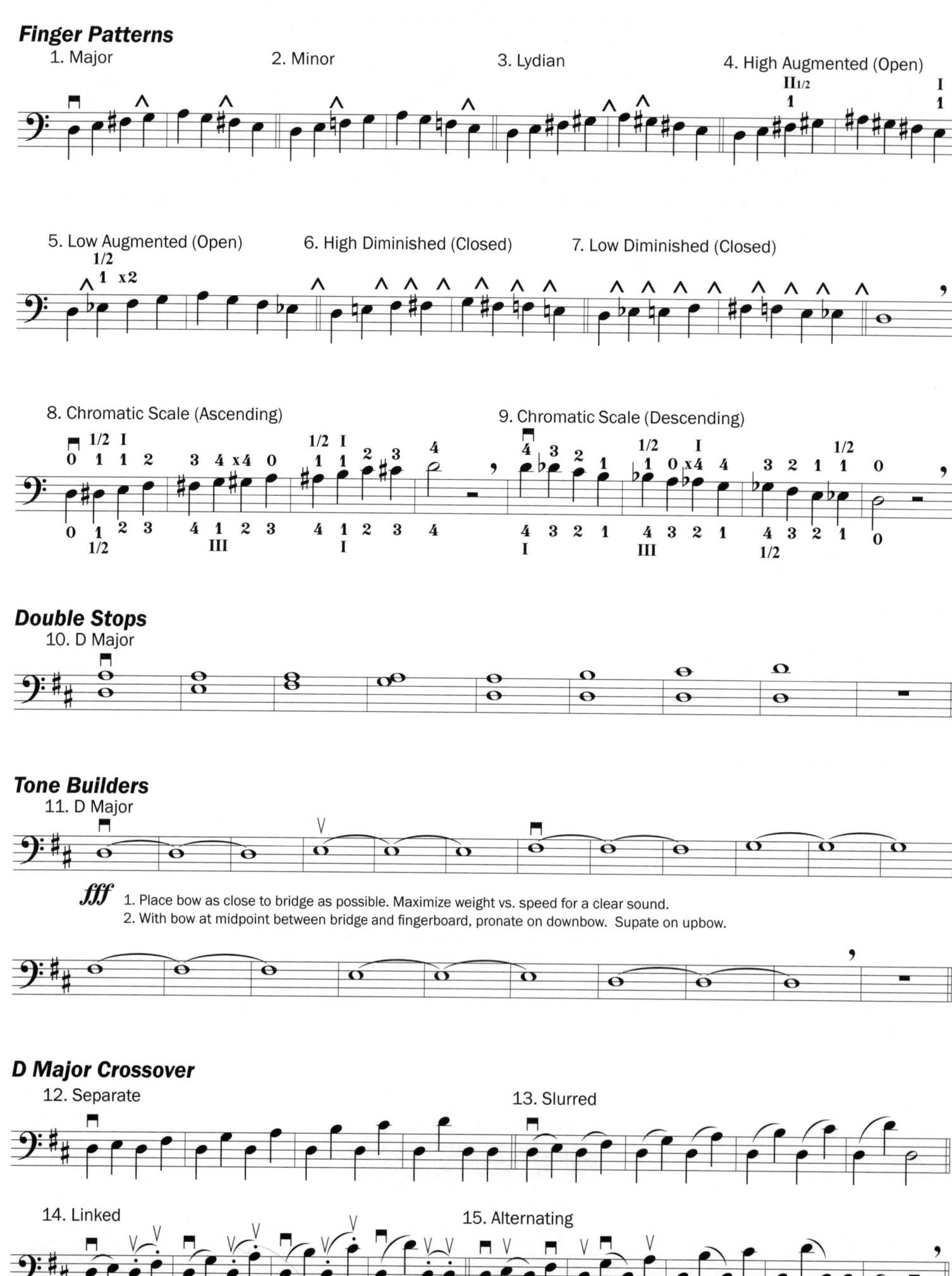

Shifting (continued)

24. Same Finger Shifts

* indicates 1st finger placement after shift

25. Low Finger to Higher Finger

* indicates 1st finger placement after shift

26. High Finger to Lower Finger

Alternate Clefs

27. Bass and Tenor

* 2nd measure is same pitch as first measure.

Playing Up an Octave

28. Thumb Position

* 2nd measure is played one octave higher than first measure.

Tenor Clef is rarely used on the C string.

Positions

29. III, III½ and IV Positions

Rhythmic Studies No. 1

Each rhythmic concept is explored for four lines.

Each line may be played independently.

Lines may be linked for a continuous review.

Rhythmic Studies No. 2

Each rhythmic concept is explored for four lines.

Each line may be played independently.

Lines may be linked for a continuous review.

Rhythmic Studies No. 3

Each rhythmic concept is explored for four lines.

Each line may be played independently.

Lines may be linked for a continuous review.

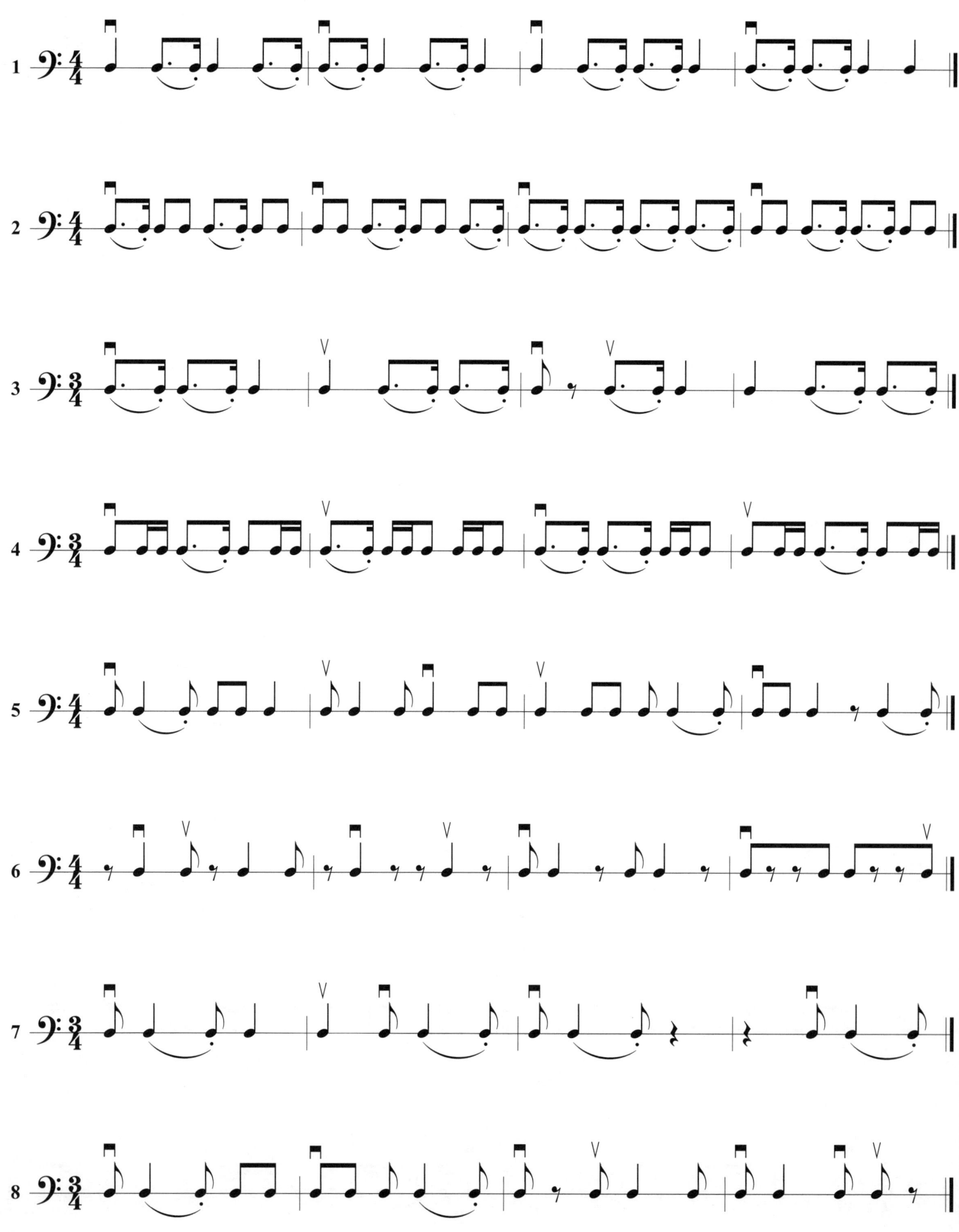

Rhythmic Studies No. 4

Each rhythmic concept is explored for four lines.

Each line may be played independently.

Lines may be linked for a continuous review.

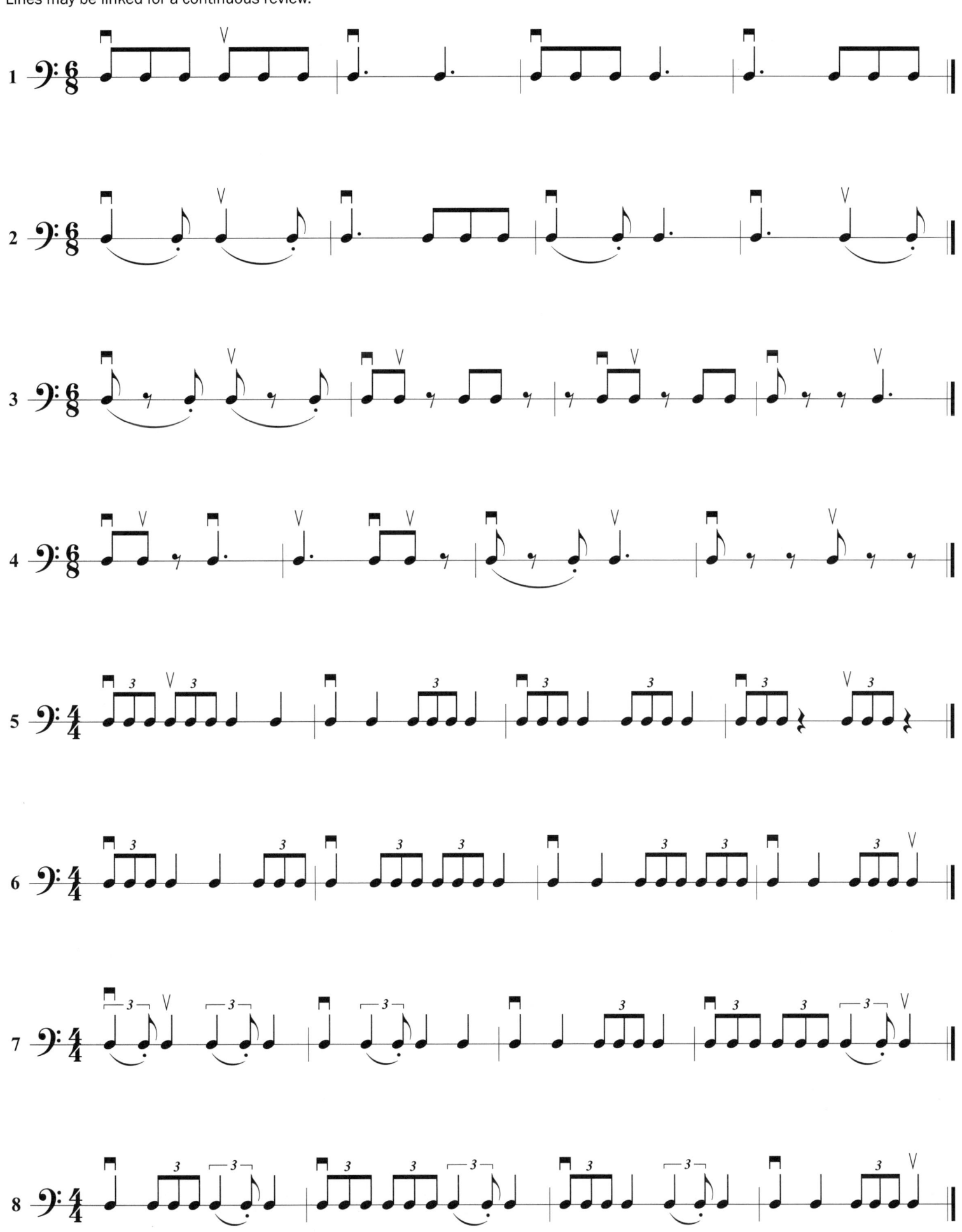

Chorale
O Welt, ich muss dich lassen

Rondeau from *Abdelazer*

Henry Purcell, England

Kreutzer Etude No. 2
from 42 Studies or Caprices for the Violin

Rodolphe Kreutzer, France
Born of German parents
Arranged by Sandra Dackow

Allegro Moderato

Shifting to Natural Harmonics

Lightly slide your 3rd finger along the string until you divide the vibrating string in half and the natural harmonic clearly sounds. Keep the frame of the hand the same and move the thumb along with the fingers. Pull a faster bow stroke on the harmonic notes.

Gavotte — F.J. Gossec, The Netherlands

More Natural Harmonics

Lightly touch the 1st finger to the string in IV position. You are dividing the string into thirds that produces a harmonic an octave plus a 5th higher than the open string. Use a fast bow near the bridge on the harmonics.

Tuning with Harmonics

Cello and String Bass players often check their tuning using harmonics. The higher pitches are easier to hear during orchestral tuning and allow the players to tune by octaves instead of fifths. This technique uses both the natural ½ string and IV position harmonics for Cello.

13

III and IV Positions

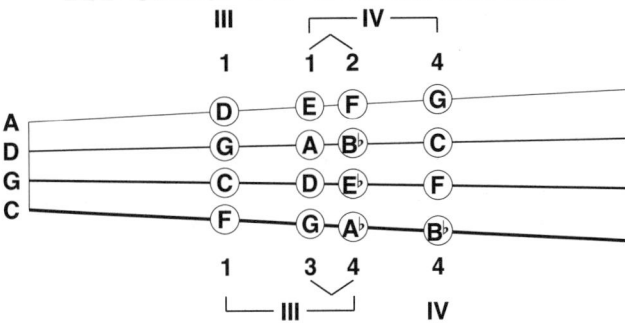

III and IV Positions

Play the first measure of each section, then sing the pattern. Replay the pattern using both positions marked in the next measure. **Play slowly and carefully.**

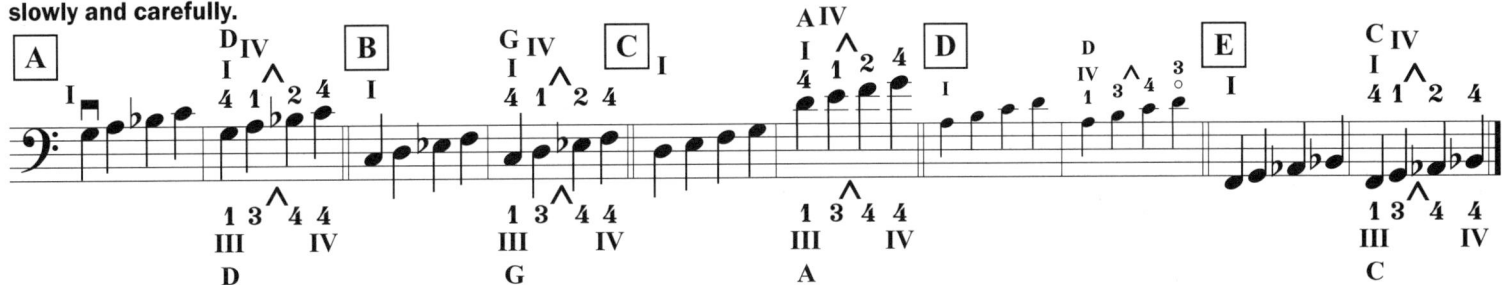

In the Bleak Midwinter - Section A

Gustav Holst, England

My Bonnie Boy - Sections A & B

English Folk Song

Shalom Chaverim (Two-Part Round*) - Sections A & C

Israeli Folk Song

Scarborough Fair - Sections A & B page 14

English Folk Song

Anaconda - Section E

French Folk Song

III, III½ and IV Positions

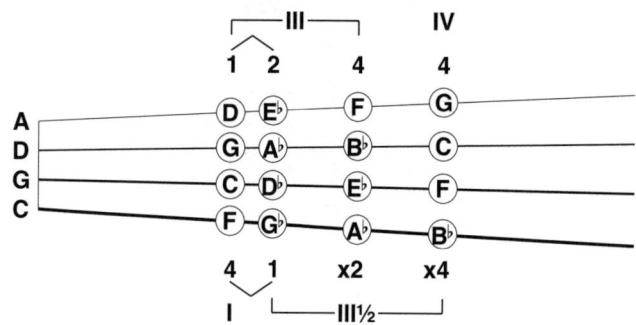

III, III½ and IV Positions

Play the first measure of each section, then sing the pattern. Replay the pattern using both positions marked in the next measure. **Play slowly and carefully.**

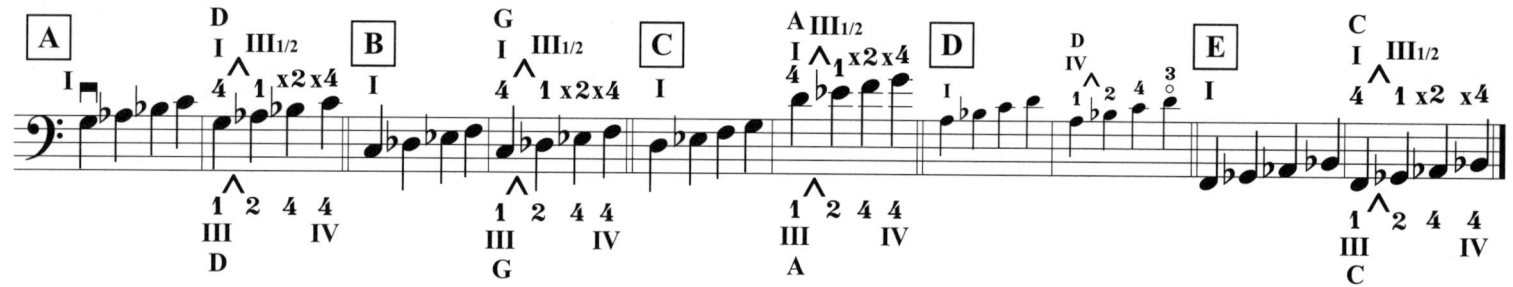

"Pilgrims' Chorus" from Tannhäuser - Sections A & B

Richard Wagner, Germany

Londonderry Air - Sections A & C

Irish Air

Turkish March - Sections A, C & D

Ludwig van Beethoven, Germany

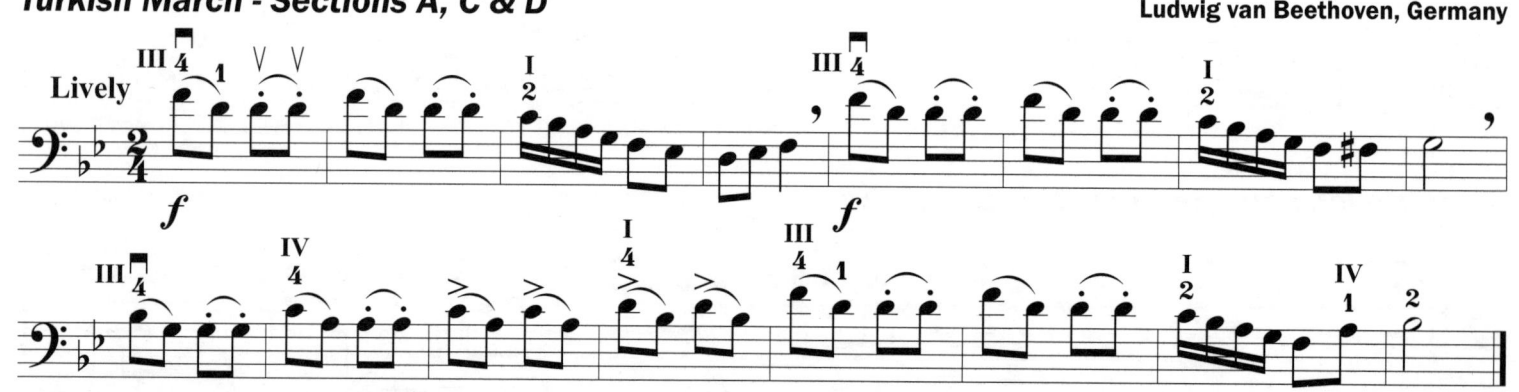

Not So Long Ago - Section E

III and IV Positions

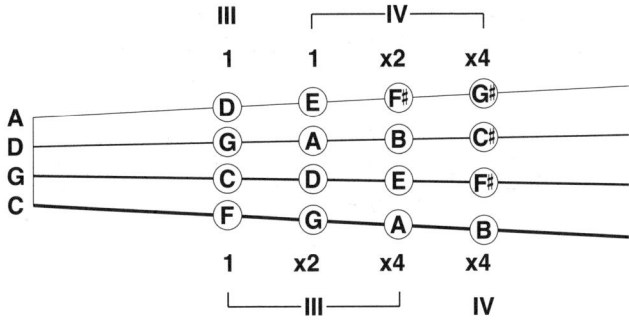

III and IV Positions

Play the first measure of each section, then sing the pattern. Replay the pattern using both positions marked in the next measure. **Play slowly and carefully.**

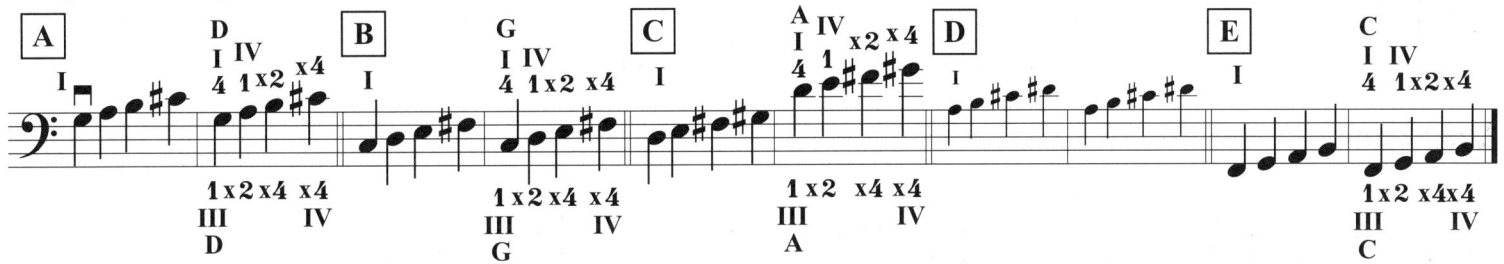

Laughing (Three-Part Round*) - Sections A & B
German Folk Song

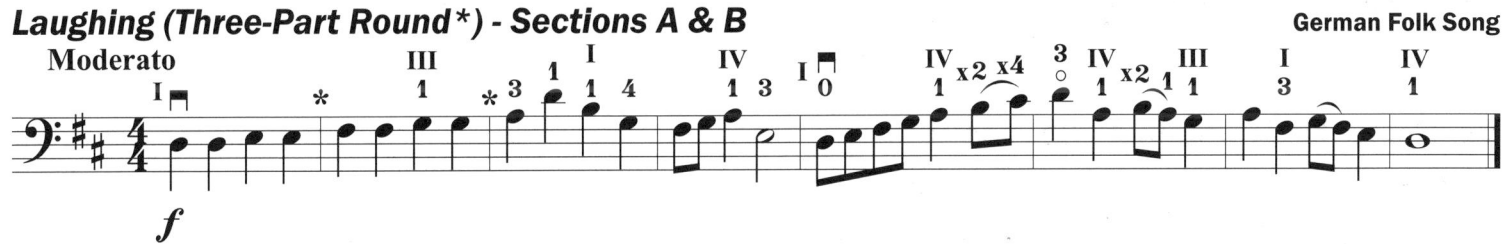

A Capital Ship - Sections A & C
American Folk Song

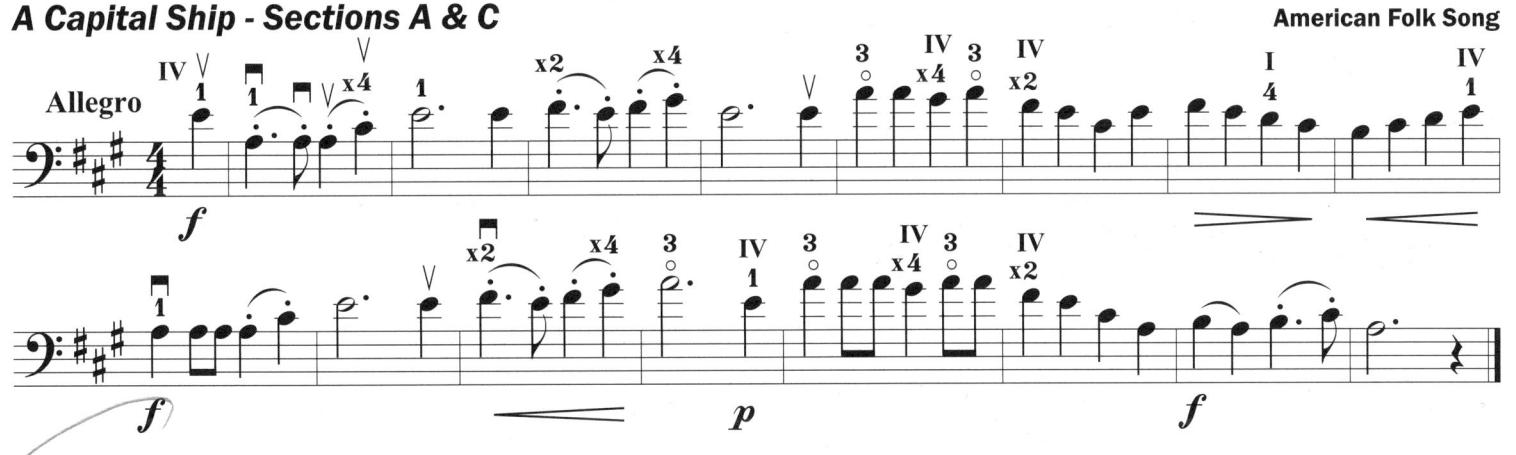

Not Really Westminster - Sections C & D

Go Down, Moses - Section E
African - American Spiritual

Theme from The Moldau

Bedrich Smetana, Czech Republic

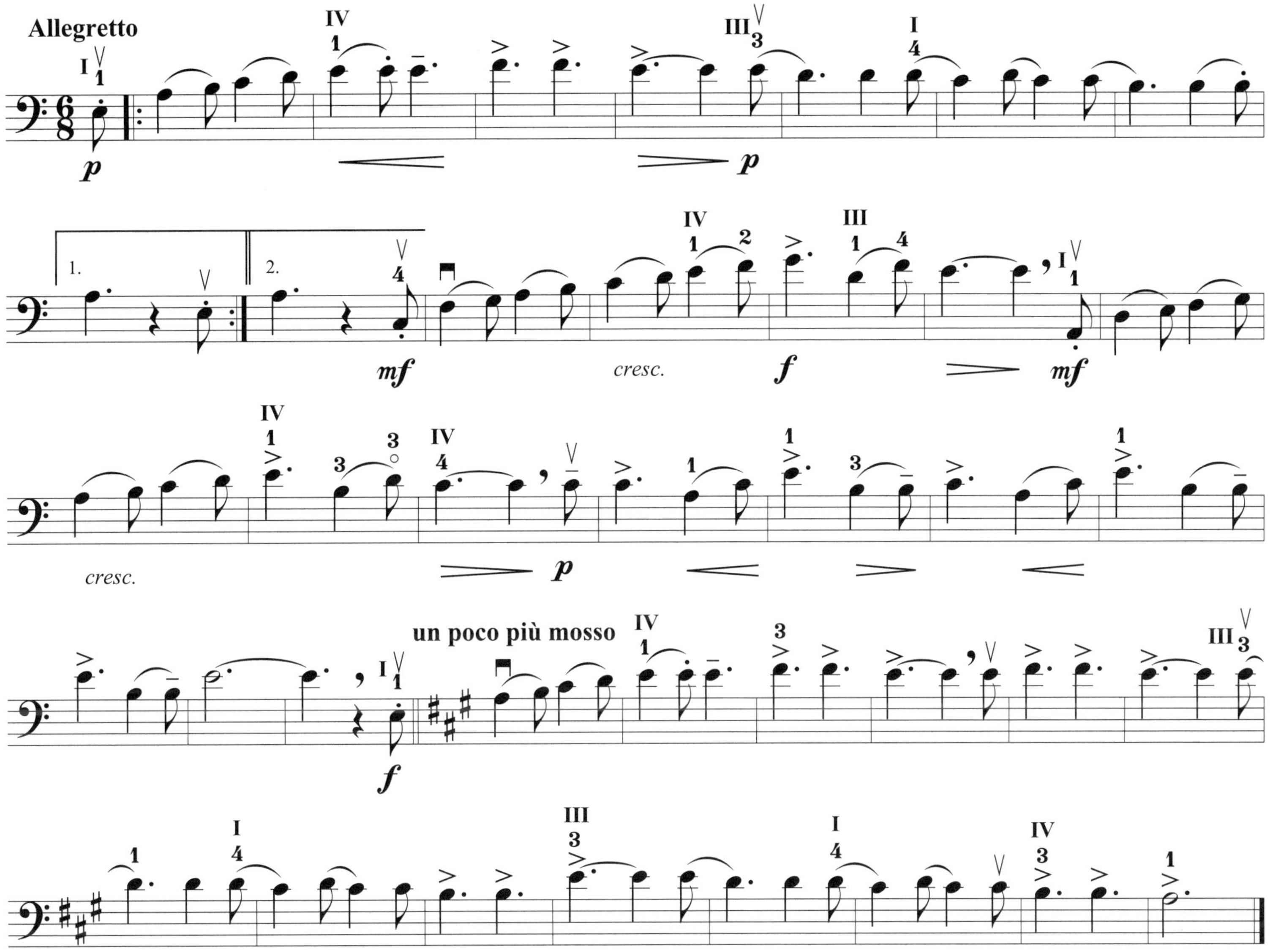

youtube.com

"Polovetsian Dances" from Prince Igor

Alexander Borodin, Russia

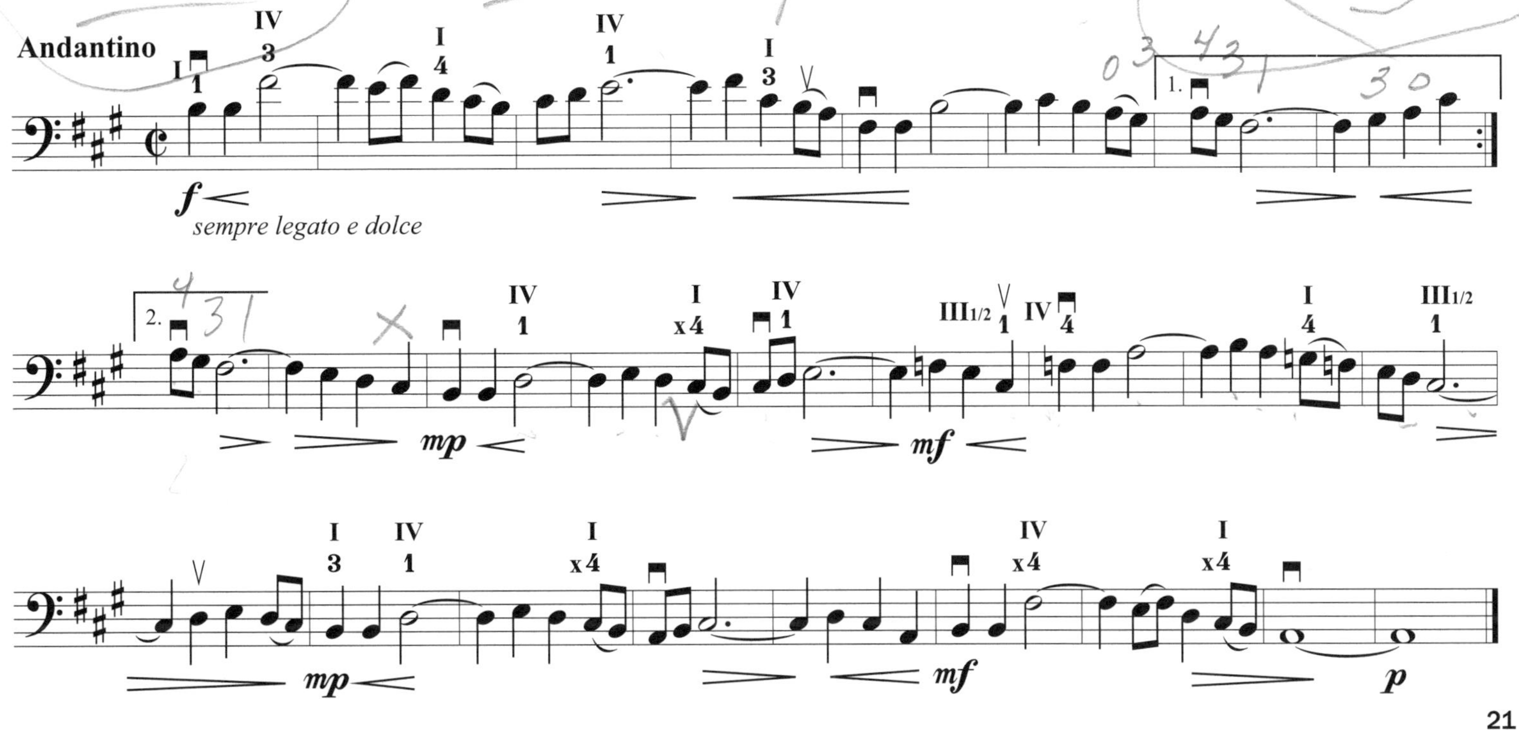

IV Position

Some compositions may include other known positions. Fingerings chosen apply to current technical development.

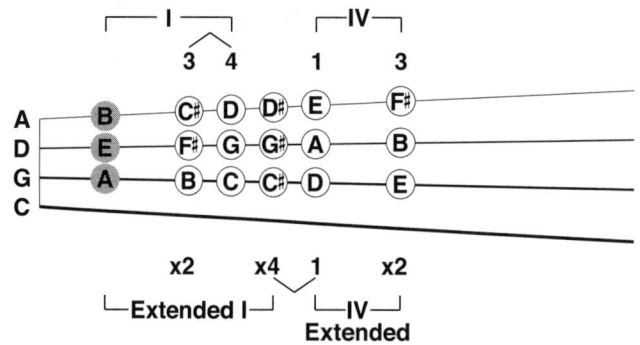

Common Finger Patterns in Sharp Keys

Useful Finger Patterns for Orchestral Music
G Major

D Major

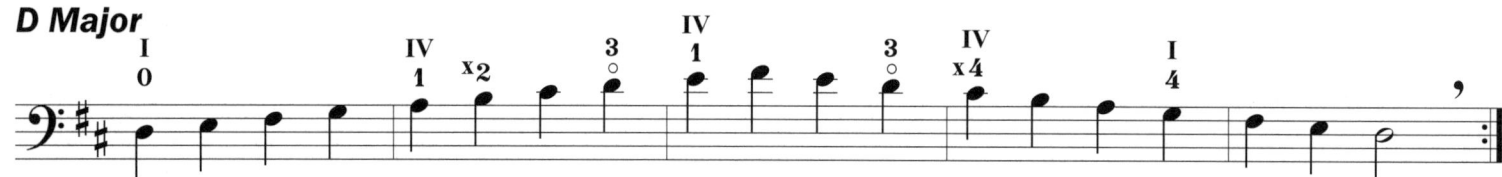

"Minuet" from Don Giovanni

W. A. Mozart, Austria

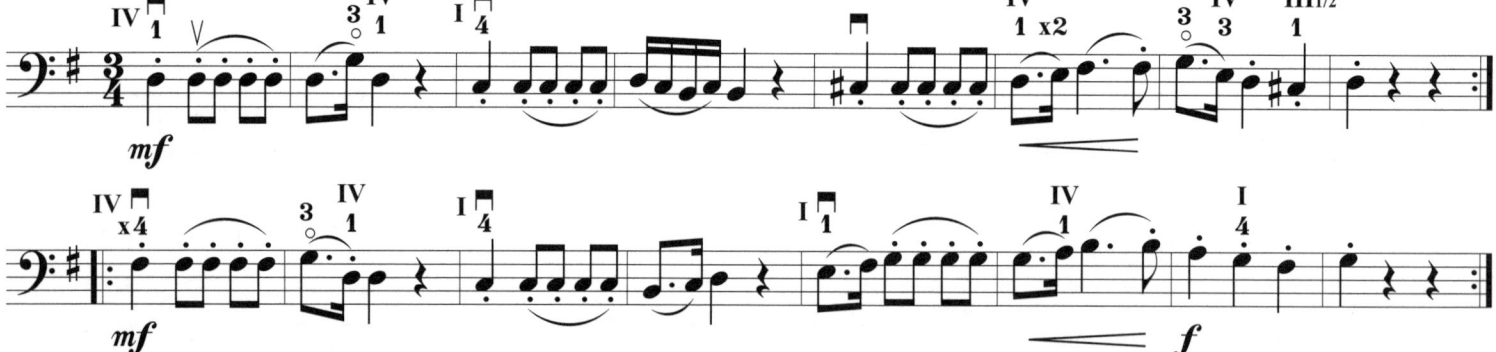

Sweet Betsy from Pike

American Folk Song

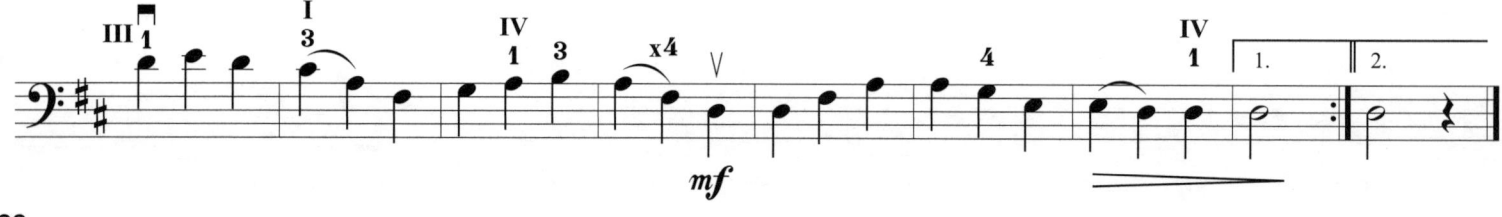

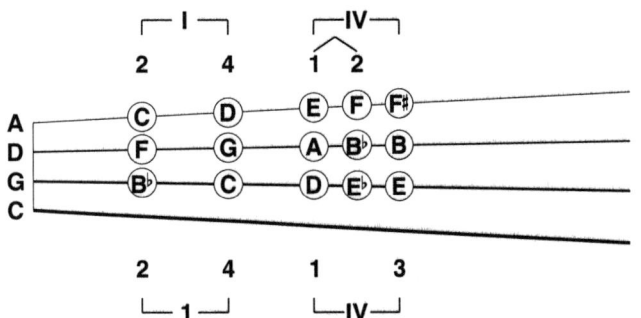

Common Finger Patterns in Flat Keys

Useful Finger Patterns for Orchestral Music
B♭ Major

F Major

On Top of Old Smokey
Appalachian Folk Song

"Intermezzo" from Cavaleria Rusticana
Pietro Mascagni, Italy

II and IV Positions

Locate 1st finger in II Position from I Position note. Some compositions may include other known positions. Fingerings chosen apply to current technical development.

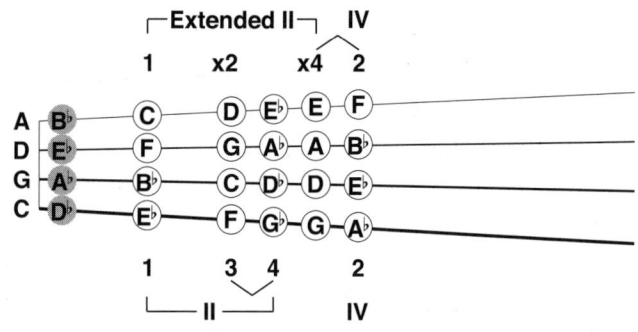

Common Finger Patterns in Flat Keys

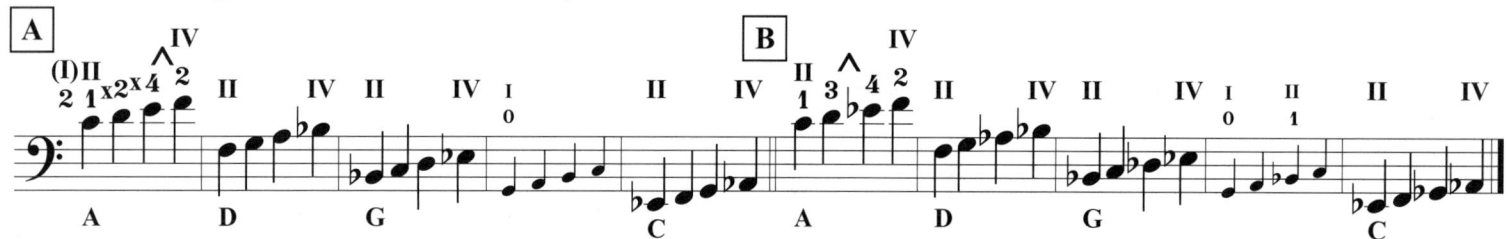

España - Section A

Emmanuel Chabrier, France

Frère Jacques (Four-Part Round*) - Section A

French Folk Song

Long, Long Ago - Section A

Thomas H. Bayly, England

Le Coq d'Or (The Golden Cockerel) - Section B

Nikolay Rimsky-Korsakov, Russia

Excerpt from Serenade for Strings (Movement 4) - Sections A & B

Pyotr Ilyich Tchaikovsky, Russia

Tune to open G before beginning.

24

II½ and IV Positions

Locate 1st finger in II½ Position from I Position note. Some compositions may include other known positions. Fingerings chosen apply to current technical development.

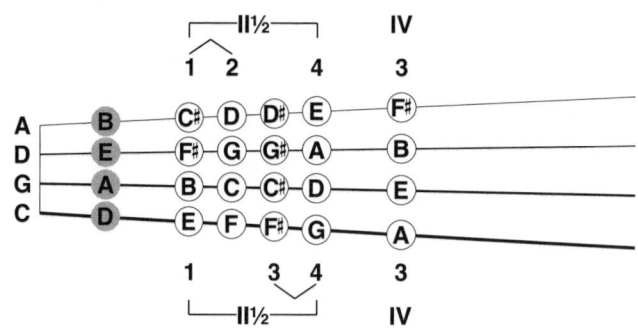

Common Finger Patterns in Sharp Keys

Minuet - Section C

Luigi Boccherini, Italy

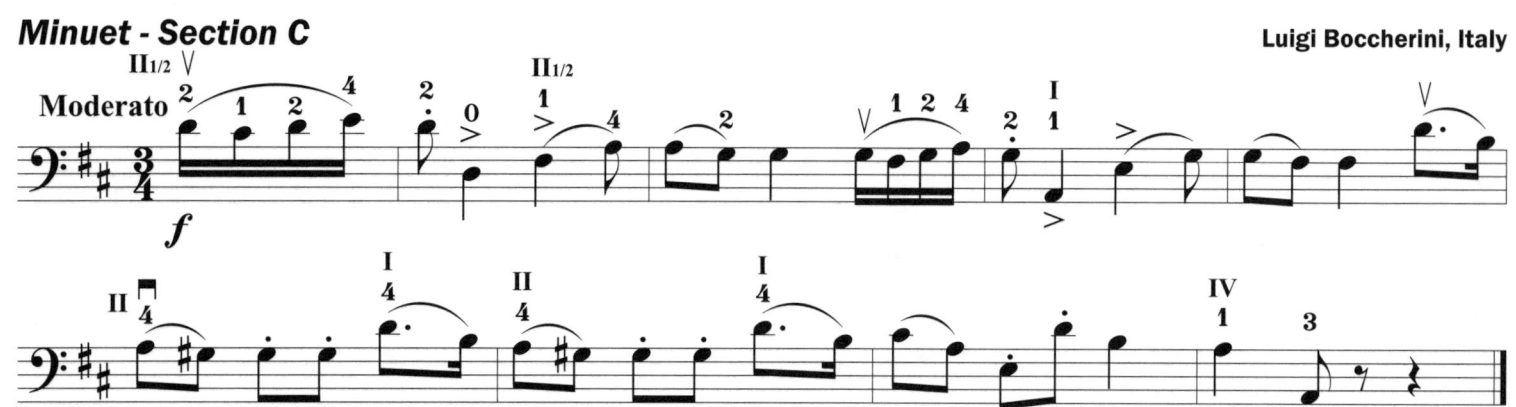

In Folk Song Style - Section C

Soloistic

Minuet from Symphony No. 97 - Section D

Franz Joseph Haydn, Austria

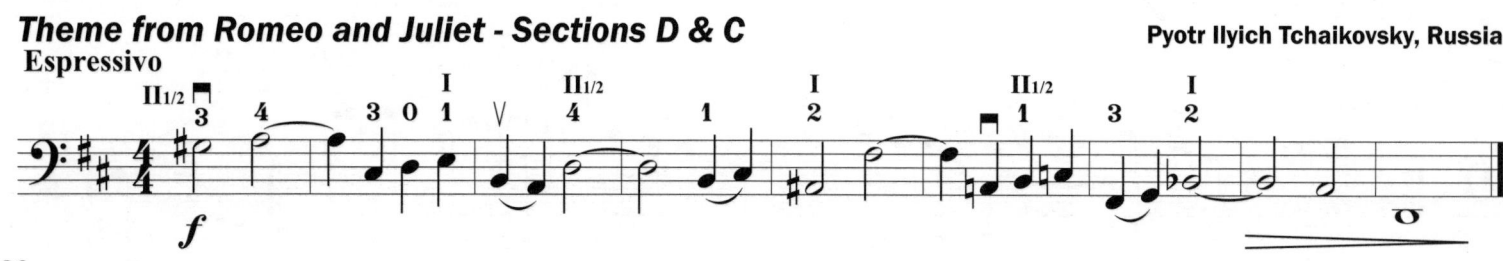

Theme from Romeo and Juliet - Sections D & C

Pyotr Ilyich Tchaikovsky, Russia

26

Cielito Lindo - Section D
Quirino Mendoza y Cortés, Mexico

La Folia
Arcangelo Corelli, Italy

"The Great Gate of Kiev" from Pictures at an Exhibition
Modest Mussorgsky, Russia

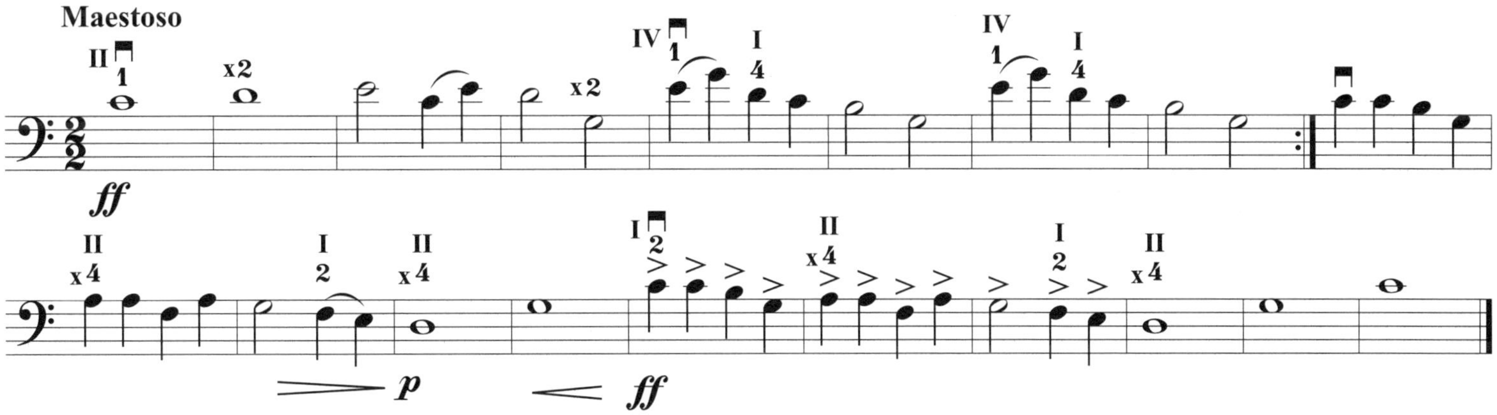

The Arkansas Traveler
Colonel Sanford C. Faulkner, USA

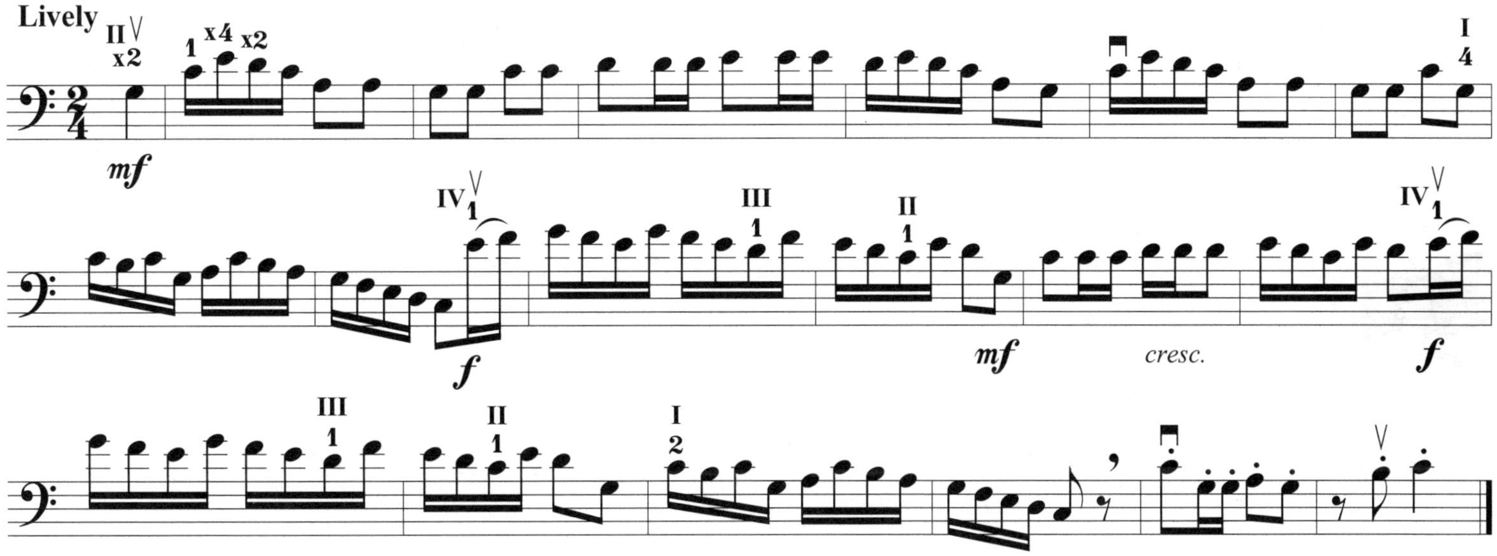

Thumb Position

Find thumb position by placing the thumb on the half-string harmonic. This will sound exactly one octave higher than the open string. Refer to the Clefs exercises on page 43 for note reading in tenor clef. To achieve proper finger placement in thumb position, the left elbow should move forward, allowing for fingers to be curved and straight down onto the string on fingertips.

Scale Building

If notes are the building blocks of music, then scales provide the blueprint for its design. Scales are built with a series of WHOLE STEPS (W) and HALF STEPS (H). Because half steps occur less frequently than whole steps in most scales, we typically mark only the half steps. This is done with a symbol (^) which illustrates that two notes "touch" each other.

In orchestral music, scales will typically take one of the following forms:

Major Scales

The **Major Scale** is built with the following series of whole steps and half steps:

```
Ascending.................Descending................
1  2  3^4  5  6  7^8^7  6  5  4^3  2  1
 W  W  H  W  W  W  H  H  W  W  W  H  W  W
```

Notice the half step between the 3rd and 4th scale degrees. The high 3rd degree defines Major tonality.

Below is the **C Major** scale.

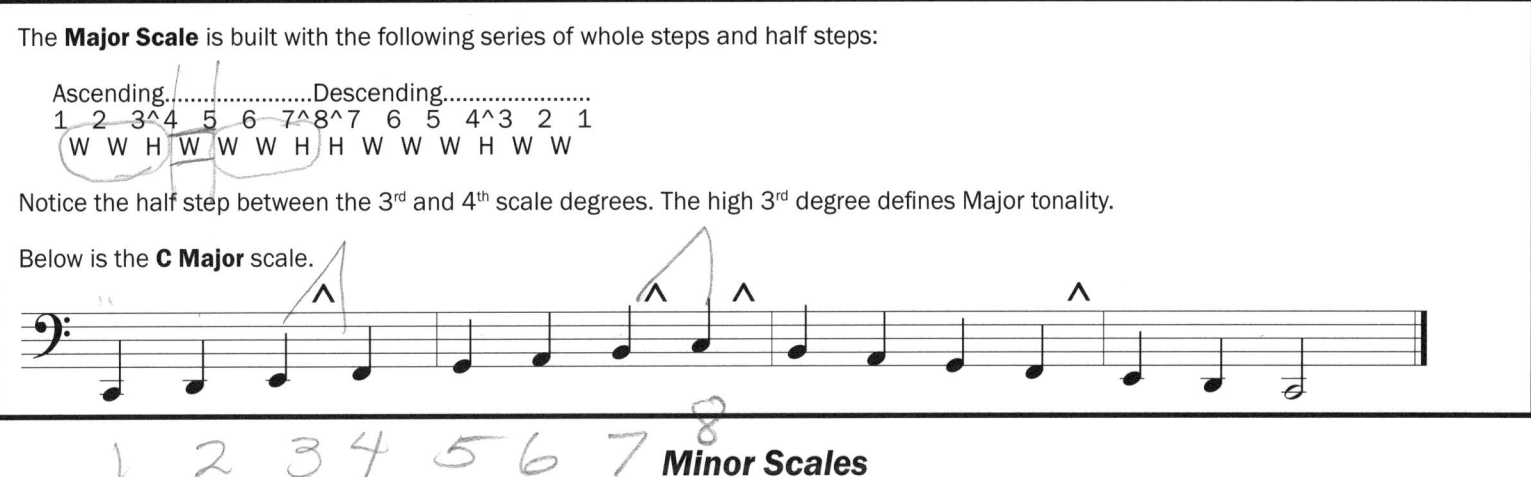

Minor Scales

There are three forms of **Minor Scales**: Natural Minor, Melodic Minor, and Harmonic Minor. The **relative minor scale** of any major scale shares the same key signature and starts on the 6th degree of the major scale.

Notice the half step between the 2nd and 3rd degrees of the scale. The low 3rd degree defines Minor tonality.

Natural Minor: No added sharps or flats; shares the same key signature as the relative major key.

```
Ascending.................Descending................
1  2^3  4  5^6  7  8  7  6^5  4  3^2  1
 W  H  W  W  H  W  W  W  H  W  W  H  W
```

Below is the **A Natural Minor** scale. Notice it shares the same key signature as C Major:

Melodic Minor: The 6th and 7th degrees of the Natural Minor scale are raised 1/2 step ascending and returned to their natural form when descending.

```
Ascending.................Descending................
1  2^3  4  5  6  7^8  7  6^5  4  3^2  1
 W  H  W  W  W  W  H  W  W  H  W  W  H
```

Below is the **A Melodic Minor** scale. Notice the altered pitches ascending and descending:

Harmonic Minor: The 7th degree of the Natural Minor Scale is raised both ascending and descending.

```
Ascending.................Descending................
1  2^3  4  5^6    7^8^7    6^5  4  3^2  1
 W  H  W  W  H  W+H  H   H  W+H  H  W  W  H
```

Below is the **A Harmonic Minor** scale. Notice the augmented second [Whole + Half step] created between the 6th and 7th degrees:

The **Parallel Minor** scale begins on the same pitch as its correlated major scale (C Minor and C Major) but takes its key signature from its relative major scale (E flat). It may appear in any of the three minor forms.

Two- and Three-Octave Scales Velocity Chart

As you play the scale, concentrate on precise intonation during the slower note values. As you gain comfort with the note spacings and finger patterns, allow your muscle memory to dominate as the velocity increases. The bow should maintain a constant speed with two metronome clicks per stroke.

Beginning tempo ♩ = 60 Increase slowly with mastery.

Continue
Continue
Continue
Continue

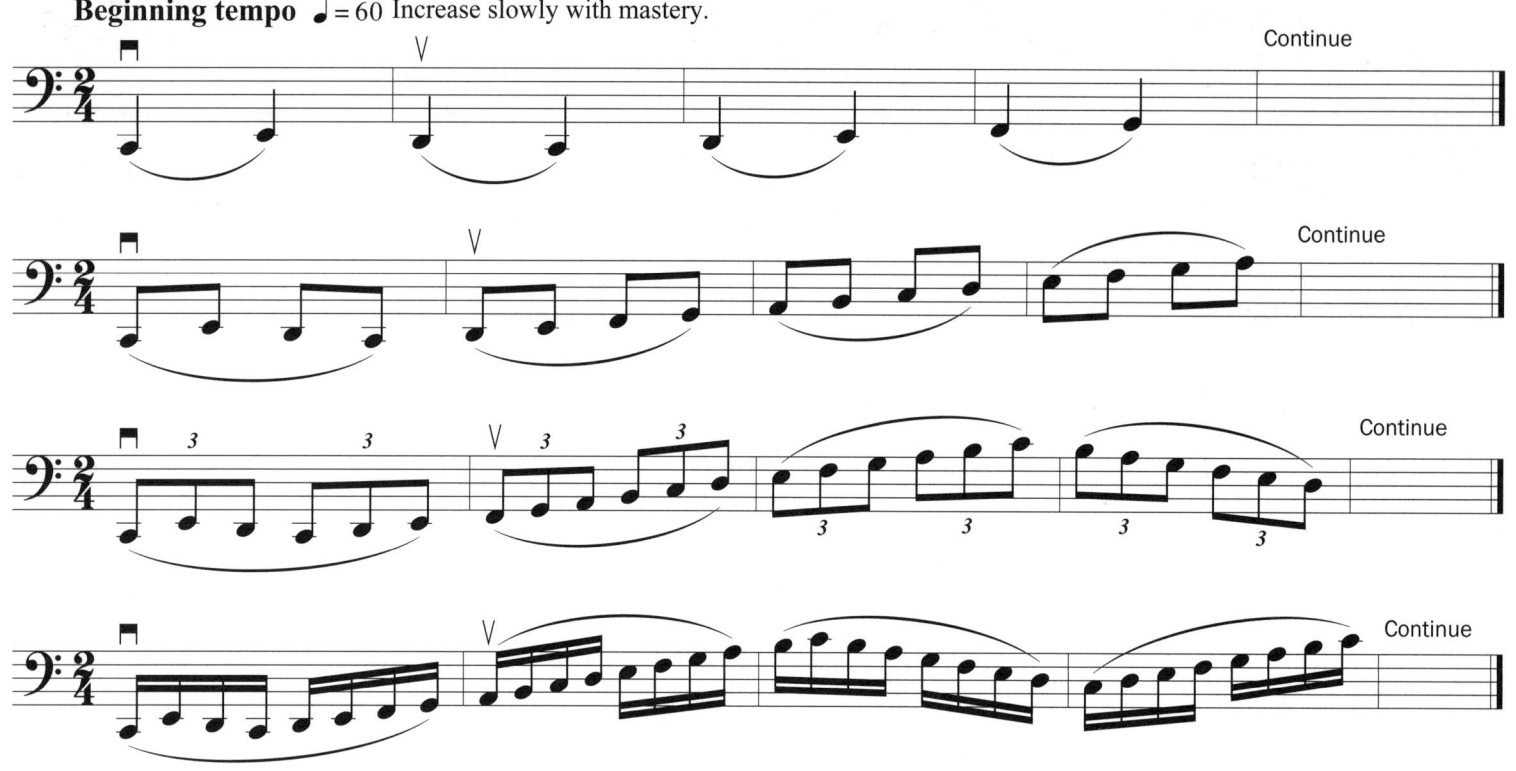

Bowing Styles for Two- and Three-Octave Scales

1. Perform one pattern on each scale pitch.
2. Perform pattern on scale pitches as they come.

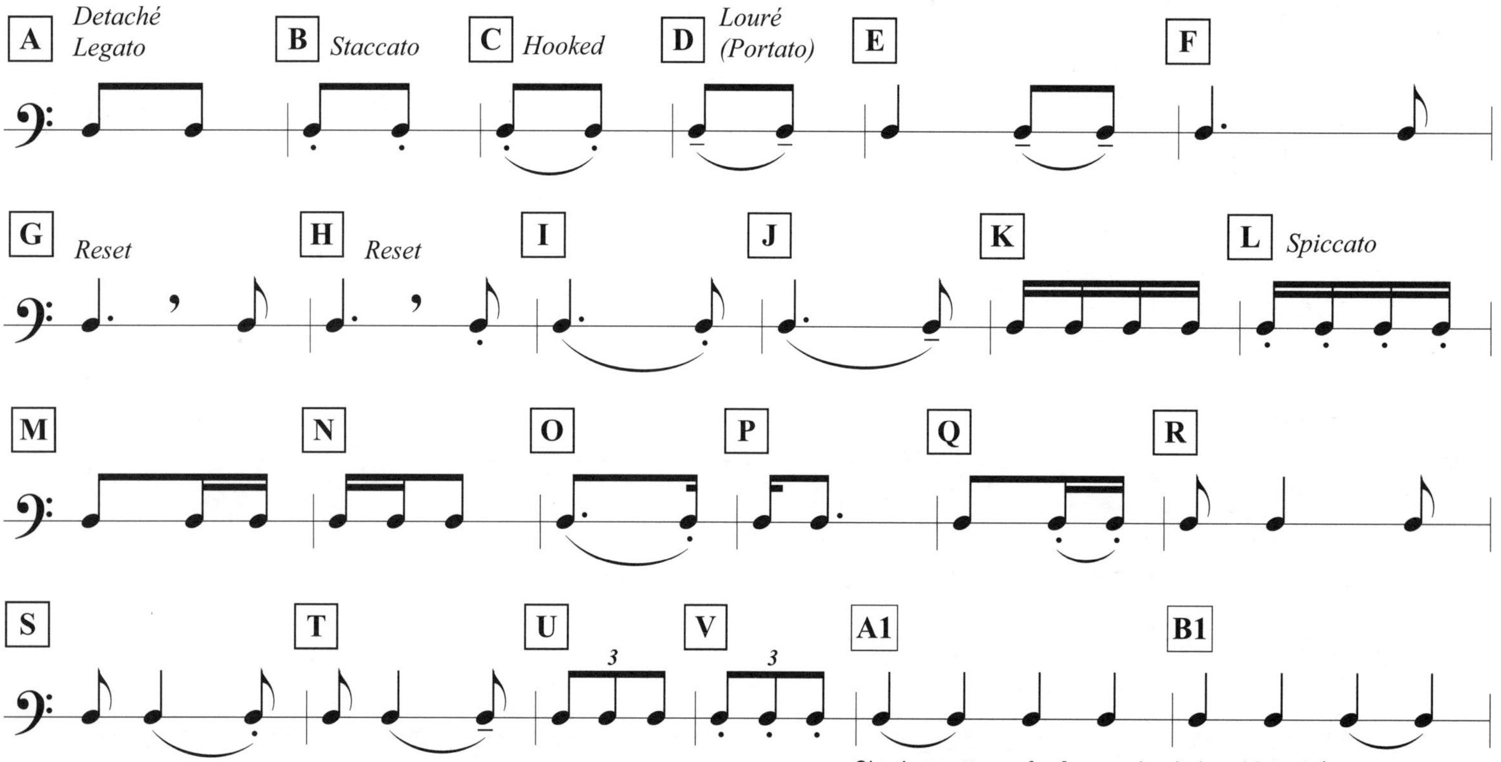
A Detaché Legato
B Staccato
C Hooked
D Louré (Portato)
E
F
G Reset
H Reset
I
J
K
L Spiccato
M
N
O
P
Q
R
S
T
U
V
A1
B1

Slurring patterns for four scale pitches (detaché, staccato, martelé used on single notes).

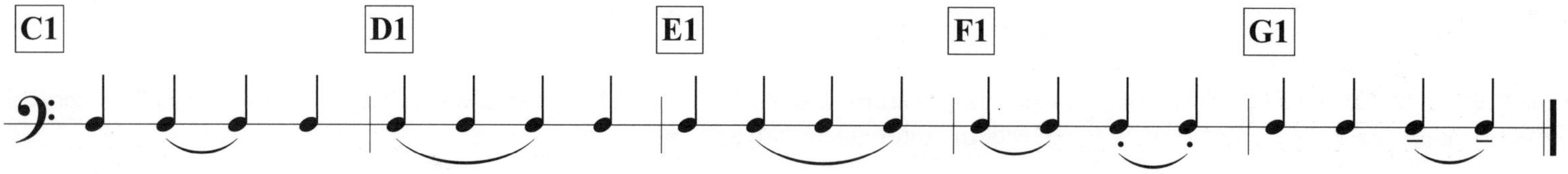
C1
D1
E1
F1
G1

Two-Octave Scales and Arpeggios

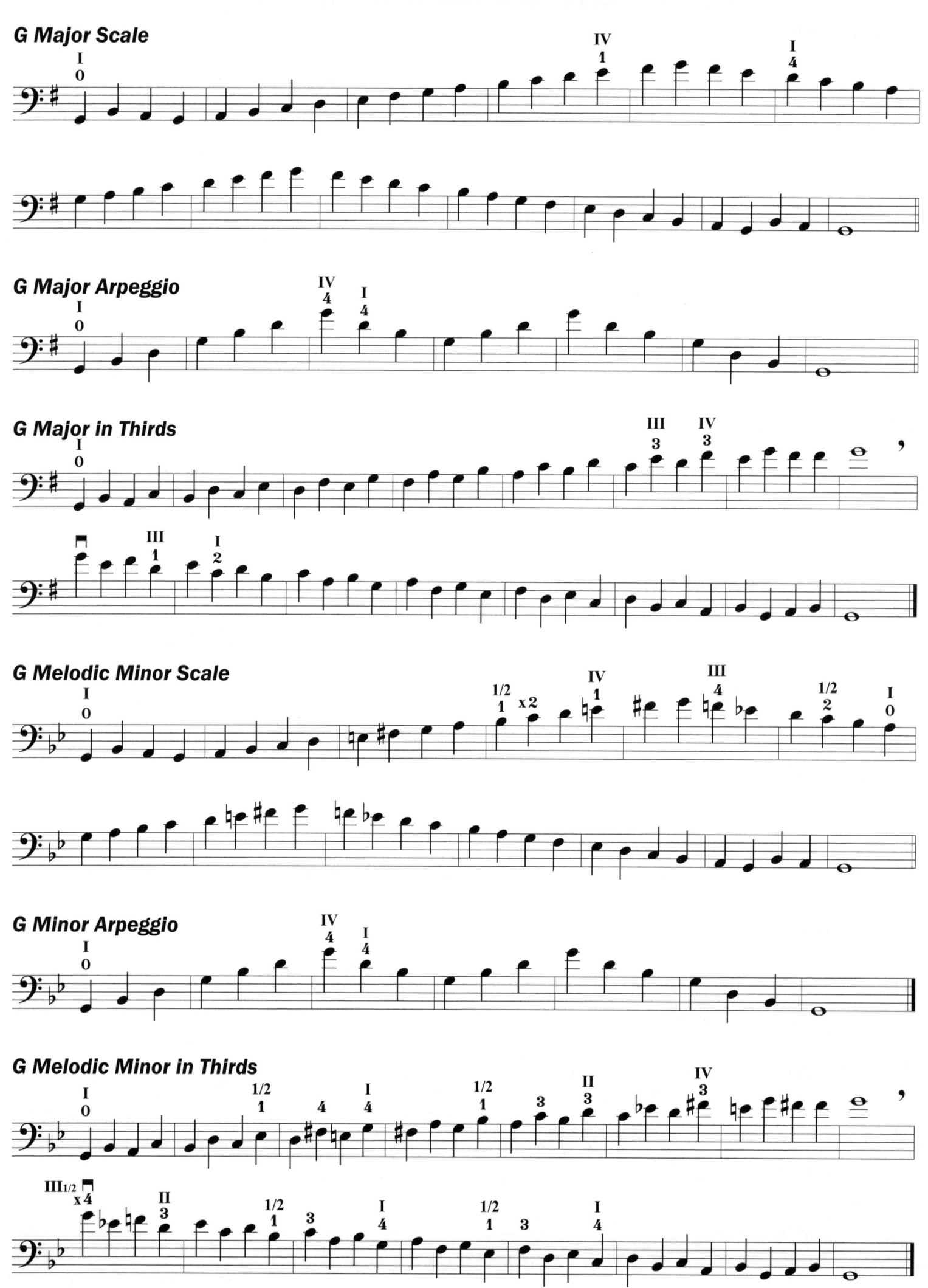

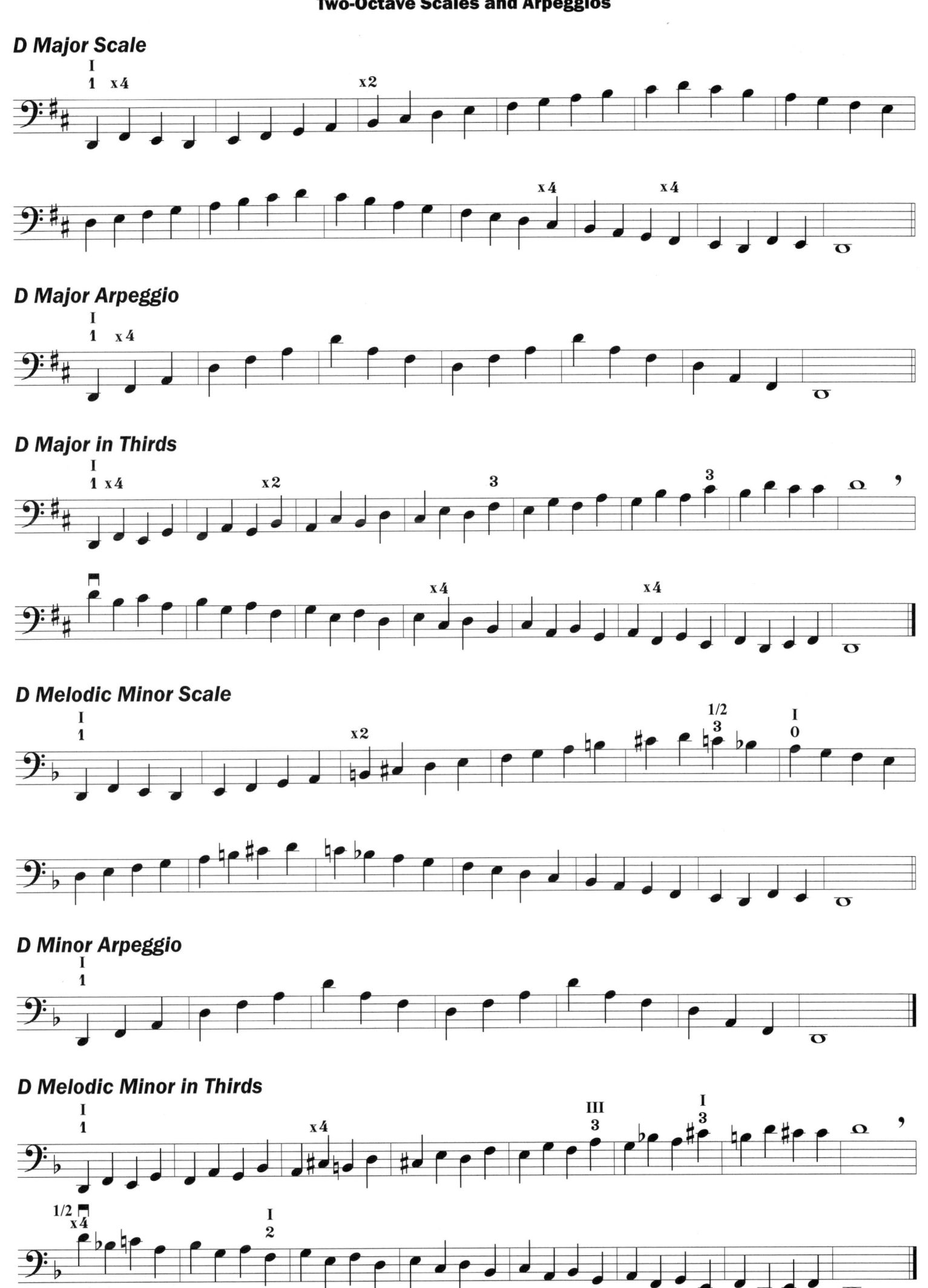

Two-Octave Scales and Arpeggios

Clefs

Scales in Thumb Position

Familiarize yourself with Thumb Position through the exercises on pages 28-30. Thumb position is found by placing the thumb on the mid-string harmonic. Fingers are added above the thumb in either half or whole steps as dictated by the key. For example, the scales below are written to be played in thumb position (both Bass and Tenor clef scales are provided for reference). The harmonic symbol (O) is used as a point of reference in order to check placement of the thumb.

G Major Scale in Thumb Position

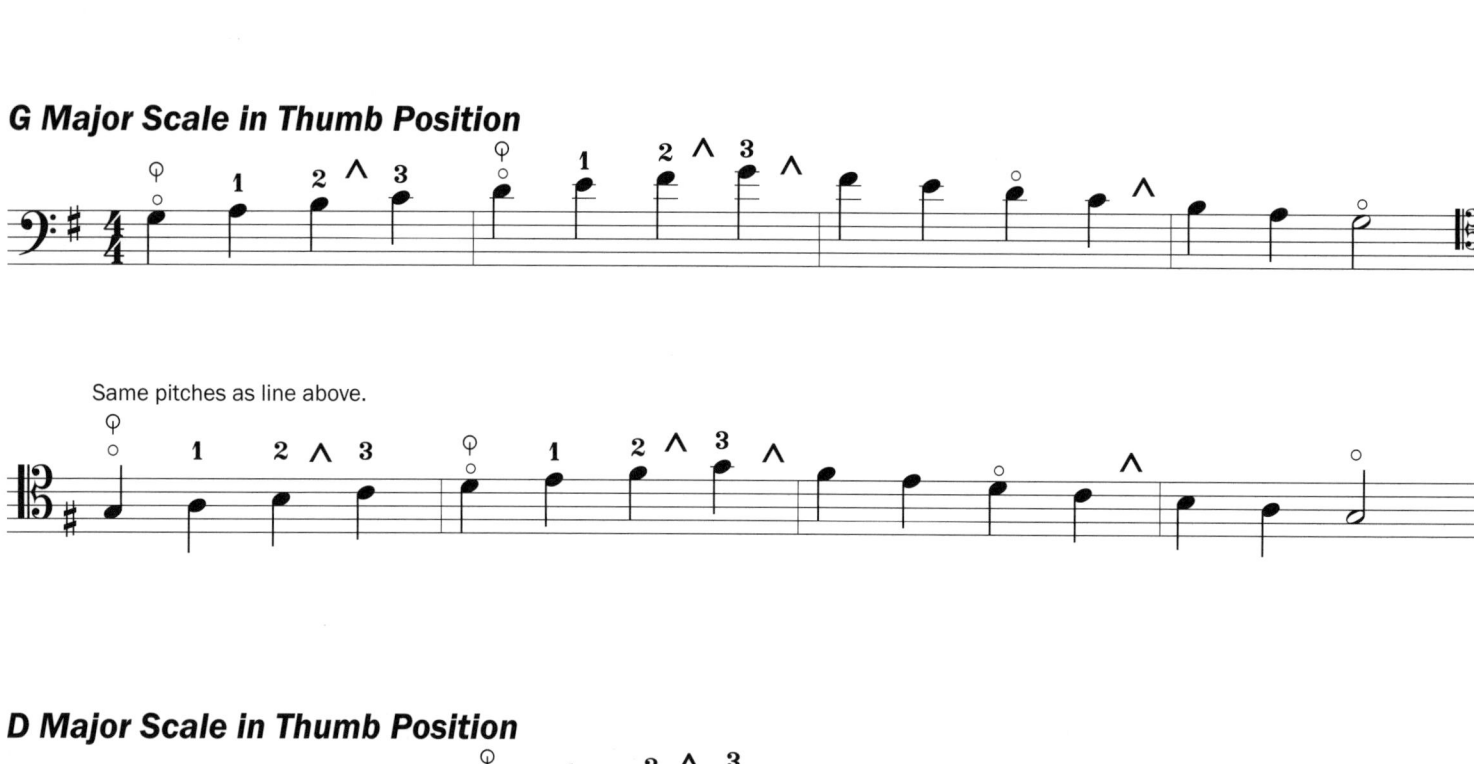

D Major Scale in Thumb Position

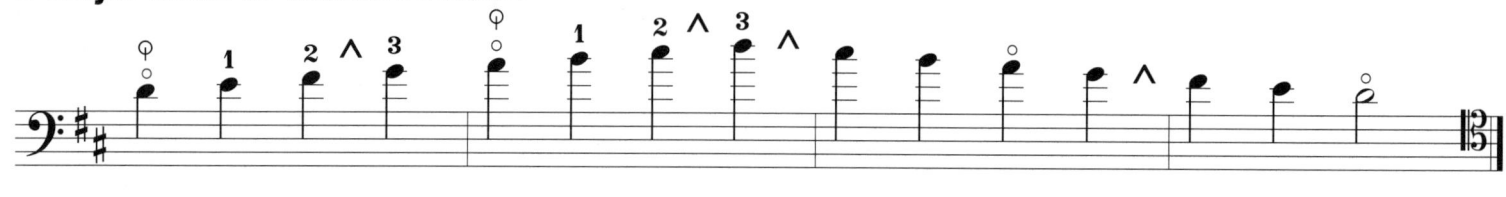

C Major Scale in Thumb Position

Three-Octave Scales and Arpeggios

The finger pattern for the third octave of all **major** scales will be: 1 x2 shift, ^1 x2 shift, 1 x2^3 | ^x2 1 shift, x2 1 shift, ^x2 1
The finger pattern for the third octave of all **minor** scales will be: 1^2 shift, 1 x2 shift, 1 x2^3 | x2 1 shift, ^x2 1 shift, 2^1
(E Melodic minor scale ends x2 1)

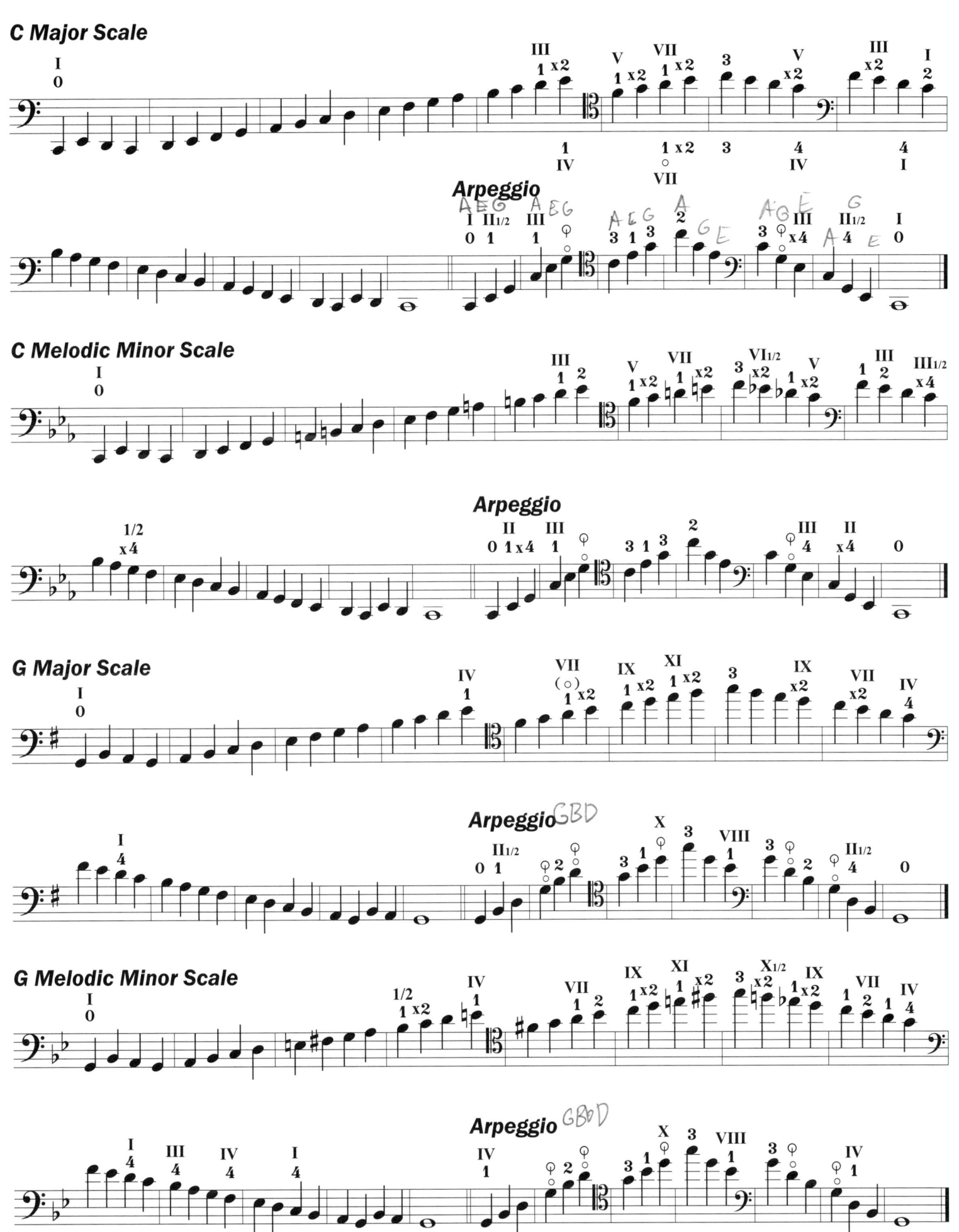

Three-Octave Scales and Arpeggios

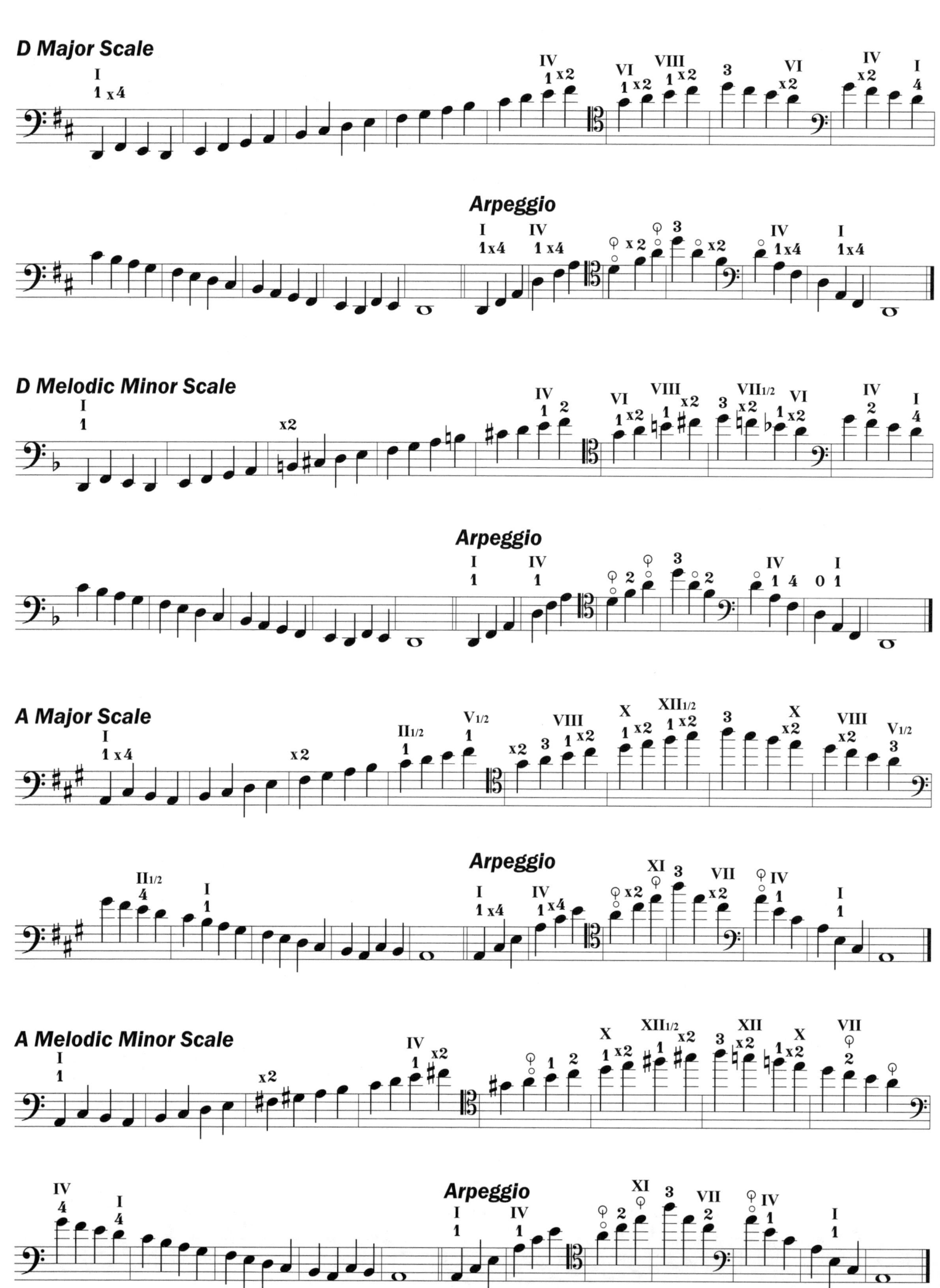

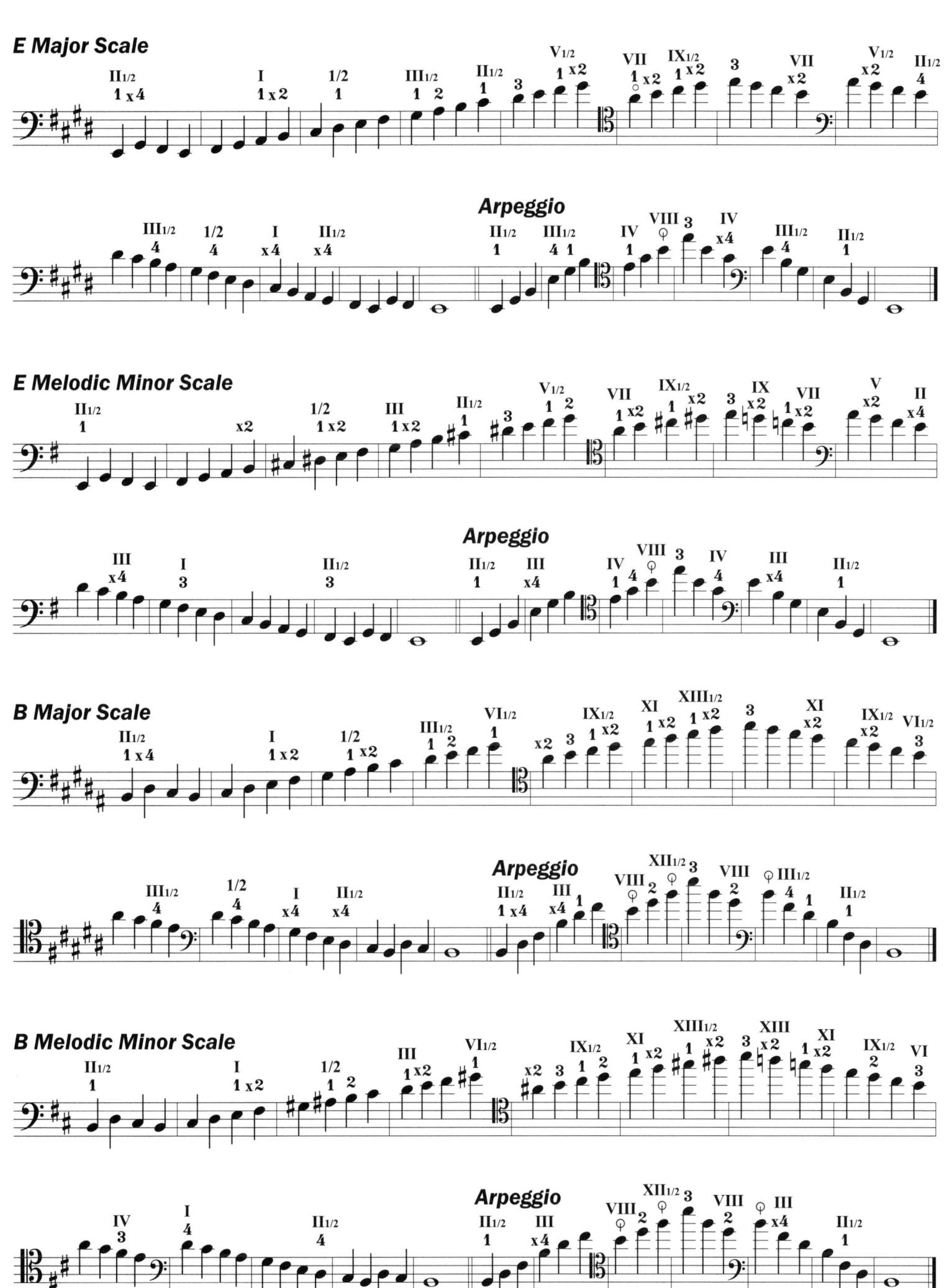

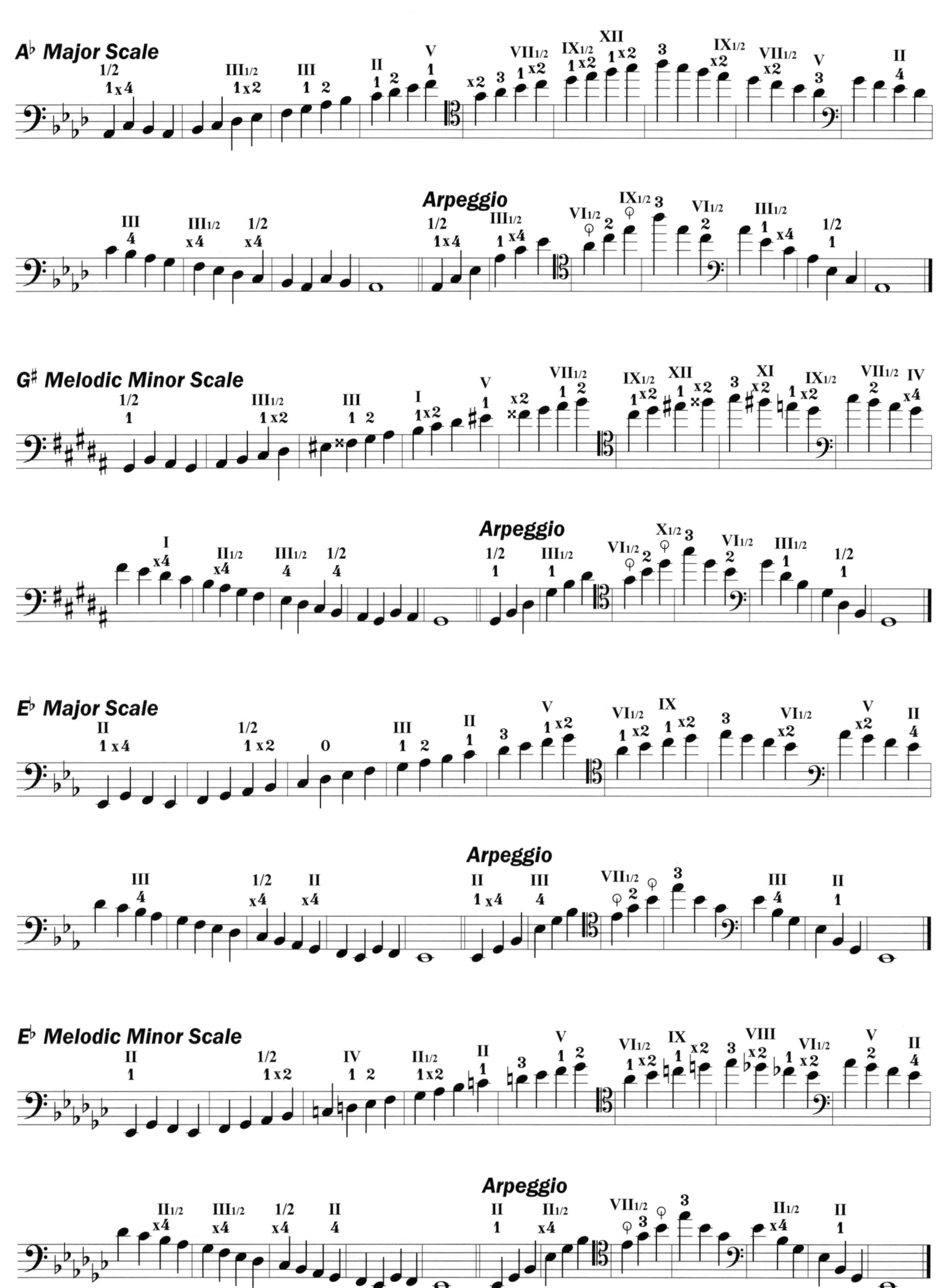

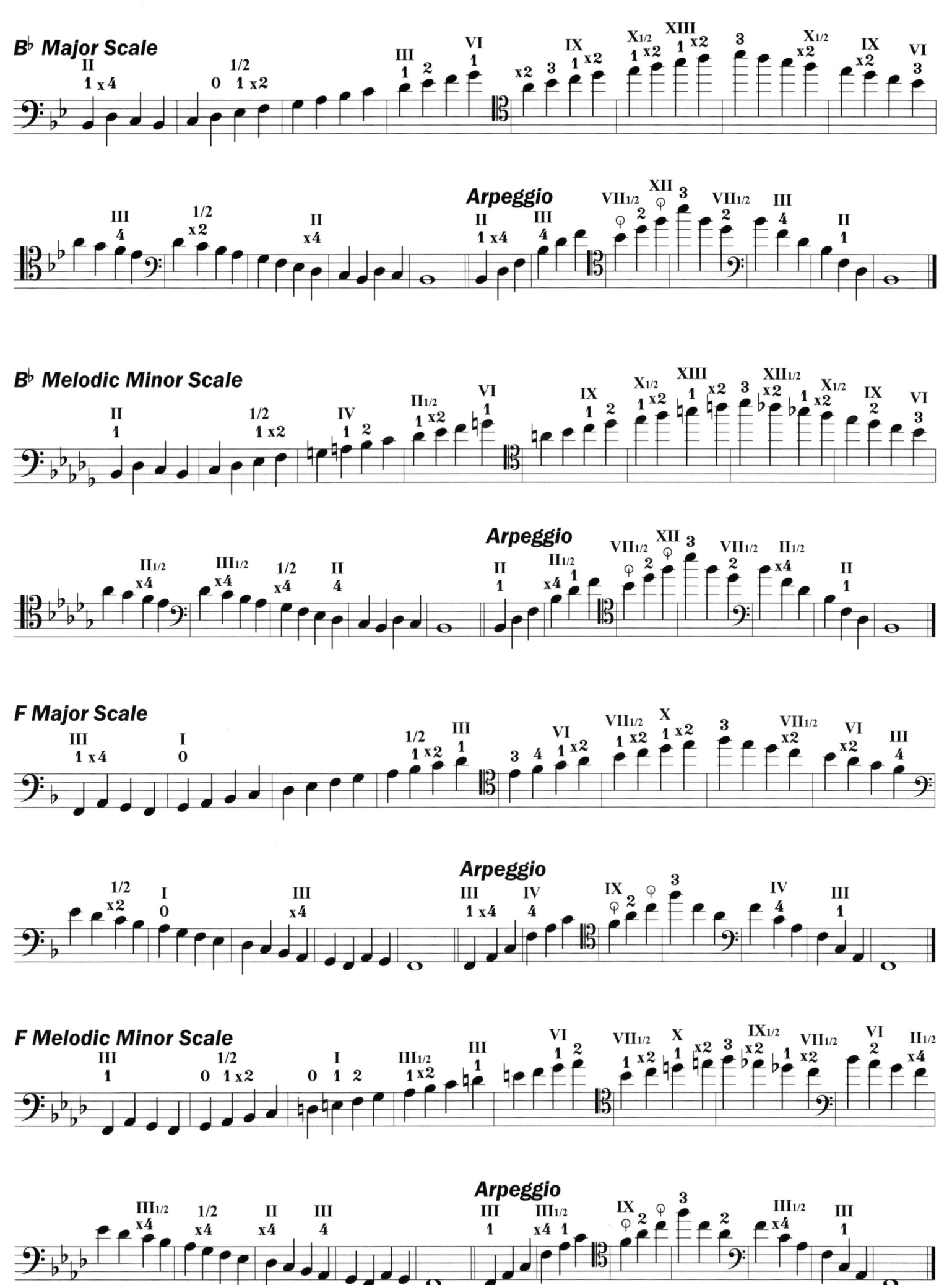

THE BAROQUE PERIOD
1600-1750

HISTORICAL SETTING
- Colonization of the North American Continent
- *Feudal systems* (Kingdoms & Principalities) flourished in Europe
- Composers employed by Church or Royalty
- Primarily sacred music written for worship

MAJOR COMPOSERS
- Arcangelo Corelli (1653-1713) Italian
- Antonio Vivaldi (1678-1741) Italian
- Georg Philipp Telemann (1681-1767) German
- Johann Sebastian Bach (1685-1750) German
- George Frideric Handel (1685-1759) German (spent most of career in England)

INSTRUMENTS
Stringed Instruments
- *Viola da Gamba* family of instruments gradually replaced by the *Violin* family as the "favorite" of composers & performers

Keyboard Instruments
- Became more developed as solo instruments
- Harpsichord in France / Organ in Germany

Ensemble Instrumentation
- Varied as to the needs of composers
- The *Baroque Orchestra* consisted primarily of strings and woodwinds
- Brass & percussion added for special effect

MAJOR STRUCTURAL FORMS
Concerto Grosso
- A four movement form (slow-fast-slow-fast)
- Sections contrast between the *concertato* (soloists) and the *ripieno* (orchestra)

Fugue
- A polyphonic composition in which similar thematic material is presented sequentially in all voices
- Employs the devices of stretto, imitation, inversion, augmentation, and diminution

STYLISTIC BOWINGS
- "Rule of the Down Bow" – nearly all stronger beats are matched with a down bow. Requires numerous re-takes of the bow with the exception of long chains of eighths and two sixteenths at faster tempos
- Faster valued notes near the frog played out of the string
- Fastest valued running notes played detaché on the string
- Slower valued notes played martelé
- Ritards at the end of compositions require greater spacing between notes

GENERAL STYLE CHARACTERISTICS
Melody
- Single melodic idea introduced early in the work
- Developed by use of *fortspinnung* (spinning out) of material
- Irregular phrases
- Structure glued together by brief returns to the main idea

Harmony
- *Figured bass* (thorough bass) used a bass line with numerical figures above it indicating chords
- A bass clef instrument played the bass line
- A keyboard instrument "realized" the figures into chords
- Passing tones and suspensions often used
- Established basic I-IV-V-I tonality and chord progressions
- Major and minor scales/keys standardized

Rhythm
- Became faster and more complex
- Continuous rhythmic drive
- Notes grouped into measures with bar lines
- Time signatures standardized

Texture
- Balance of *homophony* (melody with chordal harmony) and *polyphony* (multiple independent voices)
- Most musical interest concentrated in the outer two voices with the exception of the fugue
- Contrapuntal and sometimes irregular writing

Dynamics
- Mostly left to the discretion of the performer
- Abrupt shifts from loud to soft
- Achieved by adding or subtracting instruments

Ornamentation
- Embellishment of the music
- Ornaments introduced to create dissonance to consonance
- Most common ornaments:

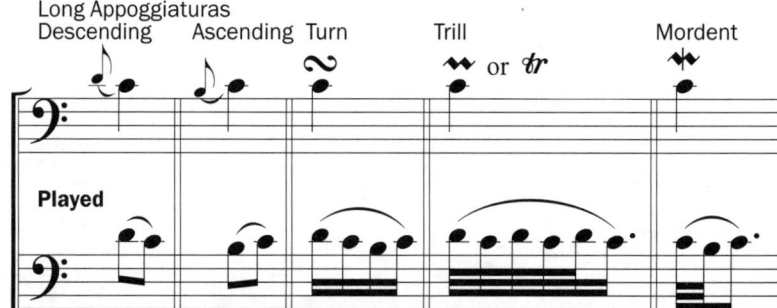

- Long appoggiatura written as a small eighth note no matter what its performance time value. It takes half the value of the note that follows it. It is played on the beat or simultaneously with the accompaniment notes
- Appoggiatura with a cross stroke did not appear in Baroque music
- All trills and mordents begin on the beat

Improvisation
- Creative use of harmonic, dynamic and rhythmic ornamentation by performer
- Figured bass embellishment over chordal structure
- Solo instrumental and vocal cadenzas

OVERALL CHARACTERISTICS
- Closely argued imitative writing
- A single musical piece tends to project a single mood or feeling (affect)

Hallelujah Chorus from Messiah

George Frideric Handel, Germany
Lived in England

THE CLASSICAL PERIOD
1750-1800

HISTORICAL SETTING
- The Age of Enlightenment begins in Europe
- Freedom of individual to think, worship, and control his own destiny
- American and French Revolutions fought
- Composers were supported through *patronage*. Employment and commissions by nobility and aristocracy
- Music composed in both sacred & secular genres

MAJOR COMPOSERS
- Christoph Willibald Gluck (1714-1787) German
- Johann Stamitz (1717-1757) Bohemian
- Franz Joseph Haydn (1732-1809) Austrian
- Francois-Joseph Gossec (1734-1829) French
- Luigi Boccherini (1743-1805) Italian
- Muzio Clementi (1752-1832) Italian
- Wolfgang Amadeus Mozart (1756-1791) Austrian
- Ignace Joseph Pleyel (1757-1831) Austrian
- Ludwig van Beethoven (1770-1827) German

INSTRUMENTS

Stringed Instruments
- *Violin* family becomes firmly established as the preferred bowed stringed instruments of the day

Keyboard Instruments
- Transition to secular music reduces the role of the *organ*
- *Harpsichord* gradually replaced by the *pianoforte*
- *Pianoforte* (forerunner of the modern piano) is the instrument of choice for soloists and composers

Ensemble Instrumentation
- Resident orchestras organized at the courts of Mannheim and Esterhazy standardized the Classical Orchestra as strings, woodwinds and brass in pairs, and percussion. Often played *symphonies* composed of four contrasting movements
- *String Quartet* (two violins, viola and cello) became the foremost type of chamber music
- The *concerto* was composed for a single soloist accompanied by an orchestra

MAJOR STRUCTURAL FORMS

Sonata Form
- ABA form of Exposition, Development, and Recapitulation
- Used as a first movement form in symphonies, string quartets and concertos

STYLISTIC BOWINGS
- In moderate to fast tempos, quarter and eighth notes are played spiccato (off the string)
- Staccato dots may not be indicated in the score
- Appoggiatura bowing used on two-note slurs
- Slurred notes followed by spiccato notes use appoggiatura with hooked up bow bowing. See String Calisthenics for these bowings (p.3)

GENERAL STYLE CHARACTERISTICS

Melody
- Short and clearly defined musical phrases. Usually 2, 4 or 8 measures in length in a contrasting "question and answer" format

Harmony
- Basic harmonic progressions are extended to key relationships as structural functions
- Chromaticism not as common as in the Baroque Period
- Emphasis placed on development of beautifully crafted melody with accompaniment

Rhythm
- Very defined and regular

Texture
- The bass line loses its leadership position
- Melody is king with all other voices providing supporting harmony

Dynamics
- Terraced dynamics introduced
- Symbols became more formalized

Ornamentation
- Trills performed in the same manner as the Baroque Period
- Appoggiatura written in its actual time. Its value is still subtracted from the value of the main note. Played on the beat
- Sixteenth note appoggiatura sometimes written as a small eighth note with a cross stroke through the flag

Improvisation
- Usually only found in the cadenzas of concertos

OVERALL CHARACTERISTICS
- Elegance, balance, proportion
- A theme framed by an accompaniment is new ideal
- A single musical piece may contain multiple, contrasting moods or expressions of feeling (affects)
- *Sturm und Drang* (literally storm and stress): a term borrowed from literary circles of the day often used to refer to the turbulent Development sections in Sonata form

Eine kleine Nachtmusik
Wolfgang Amadeus Mozart, Austria

Eine kleine Nachtmusik (continued)

THE ROMANTIC PERIOD
1800-1910

HISTORICAL SETTING
- American Civil War (1861-1865)
- Reign of Queen Victoria in England (1837-1901)
- Nationalism emerged with rise of a middle class
- Industrial Revolution began in Europe and USA
- Composers began to express their own convictions through their music
- Composers promoted by publishers, concert managers and the strength of their personalities

MAJOR COMPOSERS
- Ludwig van Beethoven (1770-1827) German
- Franz Schubert (1797-1828) Austrian
- Hector Berlioz (1803-1869) French
- Frédéric Chopin (1810-1849) Polish (lived most of adult life in Paris)
- Robert Schumann (1810-1856) German
- Giuseppe Verdi (1813-1901) Italian
- Richard Wagner (1813-1883) German
- Johannes Brahms (1833-1897) German
- Pyotr Il'yich Tchaikovsky (1840-1893) Russian
- Edvard Grieg (1843-1907) Norwegian
- Giacomo Puccini (1858-1924) Italian
- Gustav Mahler (1860-1911) Austrian
- Richard Strauss (1864-1949) German
- Jean Sibelius (1865-1957) Finnish

INSTRUMENTS
Stringed Instruments
- *Violin* family regarded as modern instruments

Keyboard Instruments
- *Piano* became a commonly acquired instrument in the middle class household

Ensemble Instrumentation
- Orchestra contained a very large string section
- Woodwind, brass and percussion sections expanded
- Instruments in extreme ranges of pitch included piccolo, tuba, contra bassoon and bass clarinet

MAJOR STRUCTURAL FORMS
Sonata
- ABA form of Exposition, Development, Recapitulation and Coda sections
- Used as a first movement form in symphonies, string quartets and concertos

Symphonic Poem (Tone Poem)
- Most sophisticated development of instrumental programmatic music (music that tells a story without text)
- Usually one movement
- Roots in dramatic theatrical works

MAJOR COMPOSITE FORMS
- Symphony
- Opera
- Concerto

STYLISTIC BOWINGS
- Long, sustained phrases require development of pronation and supination of the bow
- Use of specialized bowings: spiccato, louré, sautillé, sul ponticello, sul tasto, and ricochet
- Quick or long changes in dynamics require sophisticated levels of bow control: bow speed, placement and arm weight
- Heavy, dramatic accents require use of the hammered stroke

GENERAL STYLE CHARACTERISTICS
Melody
- Melodic themes of varying length—often fragmented
- Extreme dynamic changes
- Large leaps of pitch, and/or use of chromatics for increased harmonic tension

Harmony
- Still tonal but pushed tonality to its limits through intense chromaticism
- Major/minor tonality weakened
- Modulation to distant keys common

Rhythm
- More and more complex
- Often varied by changing the number of beats in a measure, cross-rhythms and syncopation
- Tempo often fluctuated with the use of rubato, accelerando and ritard

Texture
- All parts play important roles
- Melody often switches between voices
- Beautiful lines crafted for each part
- Melody is the strongest element but all parts are equally important

Dynamics
- Explicitly notated by the composer
- Range from *pppp* to *ffff*

Ornamentation
- Composers such as Brahms, Grieg, Liszt, Mendelssohn and Schumann adopted *trills* beginning on the main note
- *Trills* may also begin slowly and increase in speed
- Beethoven, Chopin, and Schubert held to the tradition of beginning a trill on the upper auxiliary note
- Termination notes were usually added for all composers
- *Turns* may be started on the upper auxiliary note (when the symbol appears above the note) or on the main note (when the symbol appears after the main note)
- *Mordents* disappeared from general use

Improvisation
- Found in concerto cadenzas

Vibrato
- Used to enhance the intensity and drama of the music

OVERALL CHARACTERISTICS
- Dramatic, expressive and emotional
- Tone color via instrumentation developed as a primary compositional element
- Tonality and dynamics pushed to extremes
- Folk music and legends identified native lands and heightened the trend of Nationalism

St. Paul's Suite

Gustav Holst, England

St. Paul's Suite (continued)

St. Paul's Suite (continued)

Sonata
Prelude (Largo)

Henry Eccles, England

Sonata (continued)
Corrente (Allegro)

Vibrato

Vibrato is the manipulation of pitch to add warmth and expression to music. The ultimate goal of using vibrato is to imitate the natural timbre of the adult singing voice. It is one of the ways a musician develops a "voice." The use of vibrato should be tied to the emotion found in the music performed. Music expressing sad emotions will need a wider and slower vibrato motion. Music that is of an excited nature calls for a faster, narrower vibrato motion. Vibrato is not intended as a means of masking poor intonation. Slow scale and arpeggio study should be done without vibrato for pureness of pitch relationship. The accomplished string player should be able to play with or without vibrato, as certain styles of music demand.

There are two basic components of vibrato: the depth of vibrato or amount of pitch variation (amplitude), and the speed of the vibrato or speed with which the pitch is varied (frequency).

For violin and viola, the initial motion of the vibrato should move toward the scroll of the instrument and return to the original pitch site. Starting slightly below the pitch then throwing the forearm towards the bridge activates the cello and bass vibrato.

The depth of the vibrato is measured by how far the rotated weight of the finger moves from the fingertip to the pad of the finger. The knuckles of the left hand should be strong but flexible, as they reflect the motion of the hand/wrist movement. The relaxed flexing of the first knuckle is especially important.

Exercise: To achieve such strength and flexibility, place the tips of the curved fingers on a desktop. Slowly move each fingertip back slightly into the pad of the finger and then return to the tip. Do each finger independently.

The speed of the violin/viola vibrato is determined by how slow or fast the left hand/wrist oscillates on the arm. In the case of cello/bass it is determined by how fast the arm itself moves. According to the highly respected string pedagogue Paul Rolland, the speed rate of an average artistic violin/viola vibrato is just under seven cycles per second. Cello and bass are slower because they are in lower octaves.

Exercise: To experience cycles per second, set the metronome to 104 and place 4 motions in each beat. For eight cycles per second, set the metronome at 120. If the vibrato oscillates too slowly, determine the current speed of the vibrato and slowly work up to the desired rate. It the vibrato oscillates too fast, determine the current speed and slowly work down to the desired rate. Adjust the metronome to slower settings for cello and slower still for bass.

Attaining a beautifully regulated vibrato is often complicated by too much tension in the left hand. Check the support of the instrument and determine if an additional, or different, support mechanism is needed. The left hand should not be used in supporting the instrument. It needs to be relaxed and without tension for vibrato and shifting. The left thumb should be only lightly touching the neck. Tap the thumb to release tension before attempting any vibrato exercises or motion. The first finger should not be touching the neck on the opposite side. If touching, the motion of the hand will be restricted, resulting in a tight, thin, "nanny-goat" vibrato.

Generally speaking, the larger the instrument, the wider and slower the vibrato. For violin and viola, the most commonly used vibrato is a hand/wrist motion. For cello and bass, the vibrato is generated from the forearm, as in trying to shake a watch off your wrist. The speed and depth of the vibrato also changes as the music moves from low to high. The higher the pitch, the narrower and faster the vibrato motion should be. The lower the pitch, the wider and slower the vibrato motion should be.

Cello Tuning

TIPS FOR SUCCESSFUL INDIVIDUAL TUNING

1. Use the fine tuners for most daily tuning. Do not begin tuning with the pegs unless you are more than a half step out of tune.
2. If you must use the pegs, make sure to push the peg into the peg box as it is turned.
3. Tune softly!
4. When tuning, stop the bow briefly at each bow change and listen to the tuning pitch. It becomes obvious if you are in or out of tune when you listen beyond yourself.
5. Ask yourself, "Is it my instrument that is out of tune?" The finest musicians ask themselves, "Is it me?
6. If you are having difficulty hearing your sound above the group, DO NOT PLAY LOUDER! Learn to isolate your sound by putting your ear to the scroll.
7. If you hear that you are out of tune but cannot decide whether you are sharp or flat, go either way. If you go the right direction the beats will slow down, if you go the wrong direction they will get faster. In every case, it is better to try to correct the problem than to play with an out of tune instrument.

INDIVIDUAL TUNING PROCEDURE WITH FINE TUNERS

Procedure:

1. Tuning begins with the A string, then the D, G, and C strings.
2. Listen to the reference pitch for the string you are tuning for 5 seconds and memorize it.
3. Sing the pitch on the syllable "loo"; this will help you internalize the pitch.
4. Using the upper half of the bow, play with smooth, soft bow strokes.
5. Does the string sound higher, lower, or the same as the reference pitch? Stop the bow briefly at each bow change and listen.
6. Tune softly. Are you tuning to yourself or the sound source?
7. If the pitches sound the same and they are smooth with no beats, you are probably in tune. If the pitches sound different and are rough with beats, you are probably out of tune.
   Tune the strings in this way:
   a. If the string is higher than the reference pitch, lower the pitch of the string by turning the fine tuner counter-clockwise.

   b. If the string is lower than the reference pitch, raise the pitch of the string by turning the fine tuner clockwise.

   c. If you cannot tell whether it is high or low, turn the tuner either way and it will become more obvious.
8. Continue making adjustments until the string and reference pitch sound the same.
9. Upon completing the tuning process, examine the bridge to make sure it is standing straight and centered between the inner nicks of the f-holes. A forward leaning or crooked bridge can negatively affect the sound of even a very well made instrument.

INDIVIDUAL TUNING BY FIFTHS

Advanced players of violin, viola, and cello often check their individual tuning by fifths. After mastering the performance of smooth, open string unisons, students may begin individually checking their tuning by fifths.

Procedure:
1. Listen to the reference pitch of A for five seconds. Memorize it.
2. Sing the pitch on the syllable "loo." This will help you internalize the pitch.
3. Tune the A string in unison to the reference pitch. When it is in tune, continue.
4. Play soft, smooth double-stops using the A and D strings.
5. Determine if the D string is in tune with the A string by listening for beats. Stop the bow briefly at each bow change and listen again to the tuning pitch.
6. If there are no beats present, the D string is in tune. If there are beats present, determine whether the D is too high or too low.
   Tune the strings in this way:
   a. If the D string is too high, lower the pitch of the string by turning the fine tuner counter-clockwise.

   b. If the D string is too low, raise the pitch of the string by turning the fine tuner clockwise.

7. Continue making adjustments until the beats disappear and you have a "Perfect" 5th.
8. Once the D string is in tune, play the D and G strings as double stops and check the tuning of the G string with the above procedure.
9. Finish by tuning the C string against the G string.

TUNING WITH HARMONICS

Cellists often reference harmonics for open string tuning. They are used as an additional method for checking intonation at the unison. Harmonics are produced by very lightly touching a left hand finger to the string while pulling a fast bow stroke. Once Cello 4th position has been introduced and the concept of "harmonic" is understood, harmonic tuning may begin.

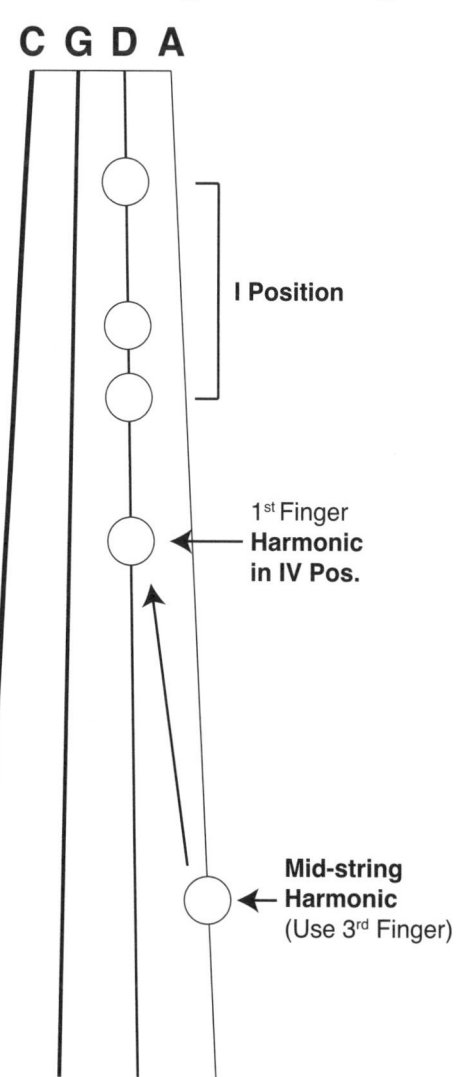

Procedure:
1. Listen to the reference pitch of A for 5 seconds. Memorize it.
2. Tune the A string in unison (or with harmonic) to the reference pitch.
3. Touch your mid-string harmonic on the A string with 3rd finger. Play it with a long, smooth bow stroke.
4. Check the tuning of the D string by touching the harmonic that lies underneath the 1st finger in 4th position on the D string. It should sound the same as the A string harmonic.
5. If the two notes do not sound the same, raise or lower the pitch of the D string until both harmonics match. Bow back and forth between the two strings with long smooth bow strokes to confirm intonation.
6. Continue the procedure by matching G to D, then C to G.

Cello Fingerboard Geography

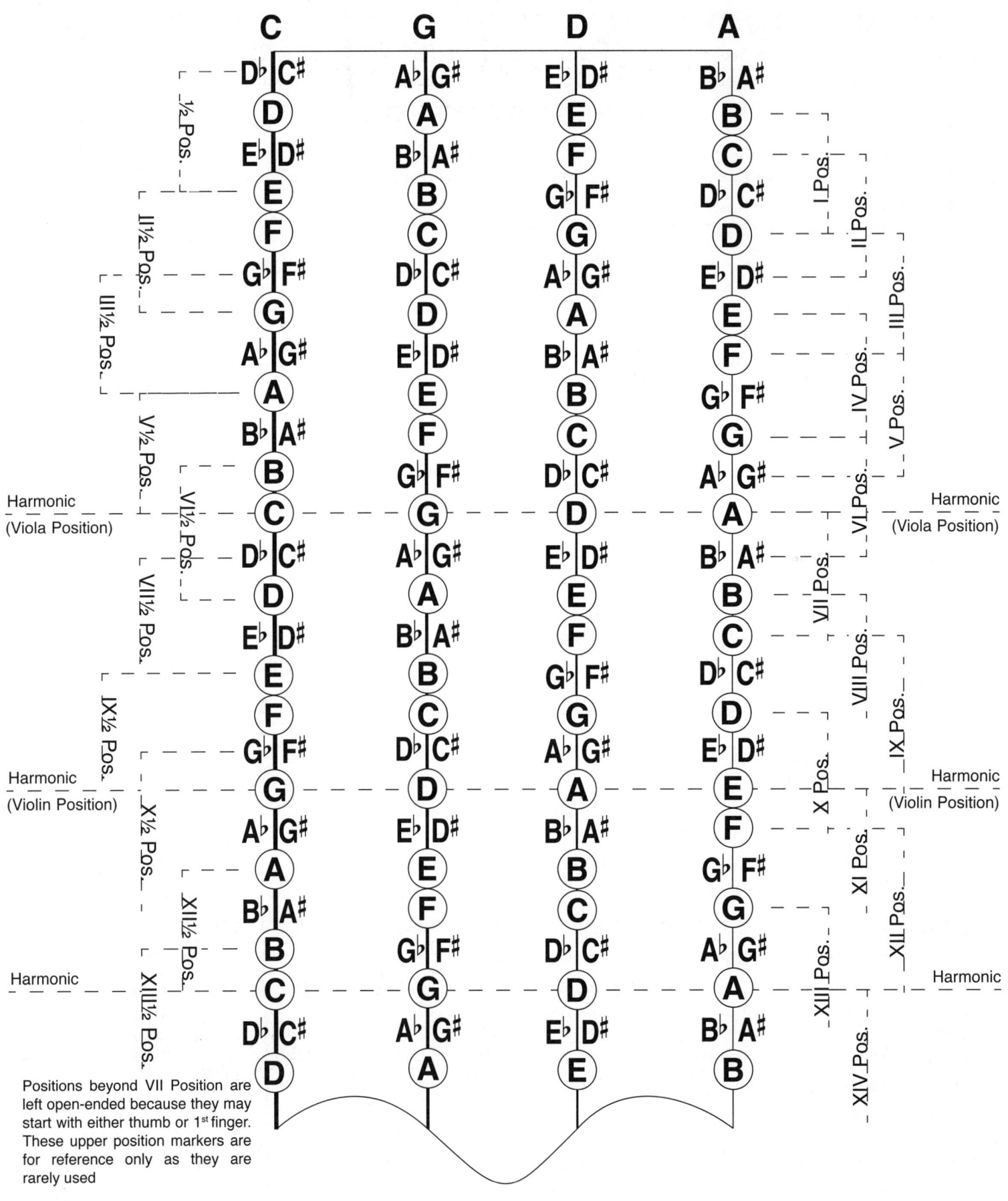